COMPUTER SECURITY: EQUIPMENT, PERSONNEL, & DATA

Edited by June-Elizabeth Thorsen

Security World Publishing Co., Inc.

Los Angeles

First Edition 1974

ISBN 0-913708-16-X
Library of Congress Catalog Card Number: 73-92473

Printed in the United States of America

FOREWORD

To a profession already rife with challenges, the computer has offered still another. To the security professional, however, the challenge must this time seem to be one that besets him, along with corporate management and the computer profession itself, with new and unusual possibilities for criminality.

Such possibilities seem limited only by the imaginations of the would-be criminals—and the counterplanning of responsible members in the computer society who, fortunately, form a majority in a rarified environment of extraordinary intellects and uncommon personalities.

To further compound a problem already difficult, opinions on computer security range from those who see electronic compromise at every terminal to those equally qualified who believe the secret lies in personnel screening, or physical protection of the facility itself, or the development of software with an uncrackable code. Or a combination of all of these.

Among the collected writings from SECURITY WORLD magazine included here, you will find all of these views and more. Herein are the best judgments of highly competent security men and computer men, functioning as consultants in security. Each position represents the total sincerity, and the best assessment, of someone outstanding in the field. Read these authors allowing for both acquisition of immediate information and the possibilities of a new viewpoint . . . and perhaps you will find that apparently divergent approaches do, indeed, have a common denominator of practical wisdom.

—— June-Elizabeth Thorsen

CONTENTS

OBVIOUS AND LESS-OBVIOUS FACTORS THAT CAN
AFFECT THE MULTIPLE INTERFACE BETWEEN
MANAGEMENT, TECHNOLOGY, AND BUSINESS
ECONOMICS ARE HIGHLIGHTED FOR THOSE WHO MAY
EVER BE CONFRONTED WITH LOSS PREVENTION
RESPONSIBILITY IN THE POLICY- OR DECISION-MAKING
PROCESS SURROUNDING A COMPUTER.

WHAT YOU SHOULD KNOW ABOUT YOUR COMPUTER AND ITS SECURITY

...an analysis by John Cosgrove *

WHAT IS DATA LOSS ALL ABOUT?

Actually, there are two ways that the computer can lose information. By accident, or by malicious intent. While the means that must be used to protect against malicious intent as opposed to accident are quite different, the person interested in computer security must remember that both losses, regardless of which way they occur, are still losses.

Few people approaching the problem of security for computers seem to remember that computerized information is so highly structured that it is stored in a manner that a human being cannot access directly. For this reason, I think it is possible that security people tend to over-weight the probability of loss due to malicious intent and under-weight the probability of other kinds of loss when they are planning computer security measures. For this same reason, I also think it is vital that security people strive to gain a genuine understanding of the computer itself.

As far as physical description goes, the computer stores its information in a magnetic imprint carried on the basic operating core, on a disc, and on the large variety of computer tapes that are run above the disc level.

That magnetic imprint can be called for from either the systems disc or the applications program tape in a variety of ways. But unless the operator knows how, unless he has the key to the program structure inside the computer—he cannot call for that information.

In other words, there is a surprisingly narrow line beyond which a company can almost lose the capability of retrieving the information it has stored. With this in mind, then, let us first consider the problems of protecting the computer against accidental loss because this is most frequent:

The first main area in which loss can occur is physical damage, *i.e.*, fire, flood, earthquake, other acts of God. The severity of damage will determine the degree to which the information is retrievable afterwards.

The second main area of loss is loss of the information, external to the

**This article was written for publication by June-Elizabeth Thorsen from an interview with Mr. Cosgrove.*

computer information, that provides control over how to get at the material stored in the computer.

A third way to lose information is through the medium itself (the magnetic tape, disc, *etc.*) actually being erased or compromised. From the standpoint of the end result, again, one is almost as bad as the other.

What we wish to do most of all is maintain the security of the information inside the computer. Corporate management and the security director must seek out experts in the computer security field to help them set up procedures to anticipate and prevent loss of information inside the computer.

It is difficult to give to non-computer people the flavor of the kind of risks that are involved in doing any kind of computer operation. And yet it is important that this flavor be transmitted, because only then can the non-computer person realize the complexities that may be involved in even simple procedures to protect the computer and its security.

WHEN KNOWLEDGE BECOMES A NUMBER

The reason for this extreme problem in loss prevention is apparent when you consider that in the computer you are now dealing with a *digital quantity*. Somebody has turned whatever it is your company knows or wants to know into a number. Therefore—from that point on—there absolutely must not *by any chance* be a compromise of what computer people call the 'integrity' of that number.

In other words, if some item of information has been turned into, say, a *five*, then that *five* must remain a *five* for all time! Because if that *five* goes to a *six*, the accidental change may make it impossible to recover any of the information in the entire storage bank. Therefore, within the computer system there should be many

crosscheck methods to protect the security of the computer information itself; and the computer must be programmed to warn the operator if a crosscheck fails.

For example, if data is being fed into the machine over telephone lines and the fidelity of transmission is poor, the computer may 'hear' that *five* as a *six*, and a chain of information loss will get started. Someone with insufficient knowledge will not perceive the problem and may go on damaging the information storage by continuing the error.

Loss of *control* of information has thus resulted, not from malicious acts, but from carelessness in qualifying the persons who are allowed to access the computer. Or, perhaps, even total failure to qualify accessing persons at all. This potential for accidental damage to a program is a greater security hazard in many companies than all kinds of criminal compromise put together!

Or perhaps you will have another kind of loss from your computer — one equally disastrous to the profits, but not permanent. For example, you may have both information and the computer system intact and undamaged — but at the moment non-operational. In such a case loss comes because the information needed is not available in a timely fashion.

The *timeliness* of much information stored in computer, *i.e.*, the ability to retrieve that information instantly on demand, is of utmost importance. In these kinds of operations, management would want instant availability to be the focus of their corporate security effort.

What kinds of reasons might cause the computer not to be operational? You may have simply lost the power to your computer service center! Or, if you have dedicated land lines traveling to your computer service center, you may find that these are temporarily non-transmitting. Or you may have mislaid some of the external information you need to access the computer and it's taking you a while to get at what you want.

Now, when I say "mislaid some information" I mean that you may have mislaid it within the computer — a bit like the *five* goes to *six* arrangement, but much less serious and quite remediable. The only problem is that it takes time, and when being available in a timely fashion is the crux of a particular computer's operation, that becomes a serious loss.

THE ECONOMICS OF OPERATIONAL HAZARDS

The point in citing the operational hazards is this: When a computer is integrated into a basic business operation, the person running the business operation, and/or the business emanating from that operation, becomes dependent on that computer. It is important for big business as well as small business to realize that this applies to both of them, just in a matter of degree.

Therefore, before any computer is integrated into an operation some questions ought to be asked. Commitment to computer use should be based on the following, "What will it mean to my operation if I lose this computer for one half-hour? For an hour? For a day? For a week? What will each of these time losses do to my whole operation?"

The more severe the results (*i.e.*, the more drastic the loss of the computer would be in the less time to his operation) the more money that business is going to have to put out in back-up systems, stand-by power, and safeguards on top of safeguards to insure that the services of that computer aren't lost for anything like the critical period of time.

Clearly, the major fear of a very large business is accidental compromise or accidental loss. For the most part, a very large operation can afford to have a greater, more extensive, and more complex set of procedures to fend off such possibilities. They can also afford specialists who do nothing but insure against accidental losses, and so a large company with a heavy operational dependence on its computer may end up with virtually total security for what they are doing.

But then we have a small company. And it may not be reasonable to say that small company must afford certain procedures, operations, and skills to keep their information from being accidentally lost. The small company may be a ten–man operation; and what typically happens in a company that size is that a secretary runs the computer data service part-time.

People in the position of this small company tend first to look for, and find, the quality of protection against accidental loss they need in a service bureau, because that's the business of the bureau. Here, the person who runs that company has made a trade-off. He does not want to chance compromising vital data, but he doesn't have a lot of alternatives.

The small businessman cannot bring in a stand-alone computer system that nobody in the shop knows how to run, and he can't afford a full-time specialist to do nothing but run the computer. He perhaps can, at most, find a part-time person to answer his needs. Realistically speaking, if such an owner understands the dependence he will have on the computer and the problems of safeguarding the computer against even normal hazards, (*i.e.*, guaranteeing the computer's security during normal running) he may have to ask himself very seriously whether he is going to get better integrity of data with a computer, or without it.

SHARED-TIME OPERATIONS —INSIDE AND OUT

Certainly it should be clear by now that if an owner (or corporate management) has integrated a computer system into the business operation to the degree that, say, something like an air line has, it would be almost unthinkable to even partly remove the ability to control what happens. Thus, for a company with this type of dependence it is no longer a question of *investment* — but merely of acquiring the proper staff and doing the job correctly to guarantee the security of the kind of access that company's operation needs to the information stored in the computer.

Even though time may be shared by a number of facilities in some companies, the computer is still accessed through ports on the premises of company property only. It is a proprietary computer. Moreover, the computer is controlled by a single position-maker who can allocate the resources of the system, and can see that it is organized so that the priorities and the needs of the business are taken into account. Once a company gets big enough for that, the opportunities for security in the computer situation are greatly improved.

For the smaller company, where computer time is being bought from an outside service, this kind of security is a much more 'iffy' proposition, of course. But then we must go back to the fact that this ten-man office does indeed have a computer terminal run only by the owner's secretary, or perhaps by one very part-time computer employee. Obviously the owner feels that it is worth the risk and he has answered all of the questions listed earlier in an affirmative fashion. That is, he has answered them insofar as he knows either the questions to ask, or where to find the answers.

TWO SIDES TO COMPUTER SECURITY

I think by now we have made very thoroughly the point that computers have built-in security headaches not at all connected to any kind of malicious act. But that does not mean that computer security in a physical sense (*i.e.*, protection against vandalism, theft, loss, *etc.*) is not also vital.

To the executive who says, "I think I may have a security problem," I have to say that computer security is a two-edged sword. One edge is always the high cost of security — and the more security, the more money.

Yet this should not go too far, because you also find out that the very existence of elaborate safeguards is an attraction! It's like posting a sign that says, "This is where my vitals are, fellows."

It is important for those responsible for security to realize that visible safeguards will attract both those with malicious motives and vandalistic intent. Further, computer programmers themselves are notorious for trying to crack any kind of safeguards, just as a challenge! Certainly anyone who has ever been around World War II type government classification remembers that the one document everyone tried to get a look at was the one with the top secret stamp on it. If you didn't stamp it, nobody would ever have noticed it. The same principle applies here.

Now — if we look at the sword from its *other* edge we can say that a multiplicity of security procedures is, in fact, harmful to the people they are supposed to be protecting. This becomes clear if we keep remembering that a computer system is in existence because it manages information more conveniently than any alternate method. What management has bought (to increase its profit edge) is the special convenience and accessibility that the computer provides.

Consider what happens to that special convenience and accessibility if (1) you have to further add to the millions put out for the computer by

(2) complicating control of its information with a lot of guards and super-elaborate system safeguards — so tightly built that (3) an employee has to cross-check himself four times before he can modify anything, and (4) he's got to have a password that changes everyday, (5) have someone personally vouch for him before he goes into the area, (6) and so on!

All of these things make the 'convenience and accessibility' of your company's information system *less* useful and *less* valuable to the operation that it is supposedly supporting. Yet that information system was bought to increase the profit dollars, not squeeze them further!

If we were to recapitulate all of the considerations just dealt with, I would guess that heavy computer security measures, if unwisely or excessively handled, can do at least two particularly profit-defeating and company-defeating things:

(1) They can highlight the genuinely valuable information so that improperly motivated people know exactly what to steal.

(2) They can create an average of a twenty-five percent loss of efficiency for the people who have to use the computer information and deal with all of the excessive safeguards.

IS THERE AN ANSWER?

What would my recommendation be? Well, if the kind of security of greatest concern to your company is malicious or criminal mischief, the *first* very best thing may be to eliminate all obvious security safeguards from around the computer itself. Concentrate on maintaining very efficiently the normal kind of procedural safeguard, which you need anyway to protect your computer information from misuse (as opposed to malicious misuse). If effectively done, the success of this may surprise you pleasantly.

It is my confirmed opinion that the best computer safeguards are not external. They are the procedural security that not only protects the information inside the computer from theft, but is also something integral to the system to guard against the forever-potential chaos that can occur if the system is in any way misused or damaged by the errors of man.

Hence, to the new computer owner I would say, "Start off with the procedural safeguards that you need anyway to run your operation right. If these are done properly they will protect it as reasonably as possible."

For example: routine (but effective) procedural safeguards will obviously allow access only to people who know what they are doing. And they will allow access in a form that permits modifying the information *only to those who are authorized*. That is a good procedural arrangement. It also happens to be convenient for security, in that it permits the individual company to also plug in its proprietary definition of authorized access.

SETTING ACCESS PARAMETERS

That brings us to the question of how access can be defined. There are several different kinds of access. We might, for example, liken it to a library, to draw an analogy. A library is in the business of actually encouraging people to access its information. Since persons using library material cannot essentially destroy it by using it, access to the information is almost unlimited in a 'using' sense.

But now consider the computer — where the user does indeed have a capability of destroying stored information or modifying it — a capability infinitely greater than in the library! You will find security data much easier to plan if you think of the hierarchies of things like this as you work to define rights of access and levels of access.

Now, add to this the possibility of dollar theft through the computer.

Then add industrial espionage, the getting of proprietary information from the computer. As security officer, you now have several good reasons for controlling the access to the computer's information, and you also have some beginning bases for defining that access — *i.e.*, deciding who should have it, and how much.

If you are a small company on a time-sharing plan, your form of library card will be a special kind of authorization number that is coded to allow you to do certain operations. If you attempt to do these things without the proper authorization, the servive bureau computer will do what we call 'trap you out', that is throw you off the system.

For the most part, software procedures that limit access do take care of securing the information both from malicious and non-malicious misuse. They apply equally well, with gradations of complexity, to either the small company on shared-time from a service bureau, or to the large company with shared-time on a central computer that is accessed over dedicated land lines from various private ports within the company's own facilities.

THE INDUSTRIAL ESPIONAGE ASPECTS

If we are going to talk about energetic, deliberate efforts at theft or computer compromise, we have a problem that seems superficially insoluble — because all it takes is one person in your own company's computer operation to compromise it. In my opinion, we are talking about company personnel as the key. I believe that personnel screening is probably the biggest concern computer security people and corporate management need have.

First of all, there is no protection from computer operations and the systems programming personnel. Once hired, they are the persons that can get at anything. There is no way around this today, and there is unlikely ever to be, because they are still the ones who have to build the systems and/or keep them running.

Secondly, something often overlooked is that these systems programmers are backed up by the hardware maintenance man — who also has to have complete access to the computer. As soon as the machine breaks down that maintenance technician must get into the system and interrogate it for an enormous amount of information. Since the hardware maintenance technician is usually supplied by an outside organization, there should be standing procedural safeguards that go into play as soon as the machine goes down.

It might, for example, be made standard procedure to immediately remove any sensitive information (*i.e.*, switch to a different disc) before the necessary maintenance work is allowed. This much safeguard is feasible for an emergency situation.

The preventive or scheduled maintenance is another matter, however. In this case, there is nothing wrong with the computer; it's merely time to clean up the tape heads, run the system diagnostics, and be sure that the machine is in order. To avoid running these diagnostics while the computer is doing its regular work, some time may be picked in the middle of the night and, say, two hours be alloted for 'PM' preventive maintenance.

When diagnostics are being run, the computer goes into a very different kind of mode. None of the normal operating systems, protections, *etc.*, are available anymore. It is like the doctor trying to find out if the patient is sick; the patient must be totally available, vulnerable, if you like, to the examination. The examiner wants to find out what is happening and he must be allowed to do so. Thus, the man who has authority for preventive maintenance is in an incredible position to compromise the computer.

So vulnerable is the computer that it is even impossible to find out how long the machine has been down! While under normal operation the computer should be programmed to keep records of all the people who access it, how long they are given areas and what areas they use, what day and time it is, and so on. But the thing that seems hard to remember is that the computer has no control over being 'down', no way of knowing what time or date it is *unless some man tells it.*

Thus, when the engineer conducting preventive maintenance tells the computer it is time to go back on operation, he starts it from some time.

When he brings it up, he tells it the date is such-and-such, the time is such-and-such; and then the computer keeps track of it from there. But it took the total control of a man to get the computer started, and no one can be sure precisely when it indeed was started. This means that there is no real check on the length of down time, as well.

PROPER SECURITY DESIGNS

Let me go back and cover once more some of the routine checks that should properly take place on access:

First, we have to understand that beyond a certain point the computer itself just can't cross-check the man. There are a number of reasons for this, one of which is that 'man' must be given the capability of getting at anything in the computer in case something goes wrong. (And that happens frequently, by the way.)

Second, what the computer *can* do is keep a record of the access. In the event that people seem to be excessively using areas not judged proportionally important to their need to know, the security officer could observe that on the computer log; and that would represent a useful protective device.

Third, both management *and* the security officer have to keep remembering, above all, to put dollar figures on the kinds of things that are useful and valuable. To think warily in terms of both the economics and the visibility. And, after that, ask whether it is worth investing what the company must — over and above the cost of keeping it running for the job it has to do — to create many duplicate safeguards.

Question intelligently the value of security return for dollars added to cost. *Remember* that the more complexities added to a computer over and above the basics needed to keep it running for purposes of the company, the more costly the computer operation is for the people who are supposed to use it.

Question the pros and cons of visibility as another important security aspect. Management may feel better with more, and more visible, safeguards. But the wise security officer knows that the more safeguards there are, and the more obvious these safeguards become, the more attractive it is for somebody to circumvent them. And the more someone might think something there is worth getting at.

John Cosgrove

Located in Playa del Rey, California, Mr. Cosgrove is a consultant in computer systems and software whose career has led him through the complexities of real-time programming, digital system hardware and software interface, on-line digital control, data acquisition and telemetry, automatic test, and other aspects of computer technology involved in computer security as well. ——→

During more than thirteen years in electronic systems, his design and implementation of computer systems and related solutions has been called upon to answer a spread of needs from aerospace to law enforcement communications networks.

A product of the Engineering Executive Program at UCLA, Mr. Cosgrove also has a BSEE from Loyola University, Los Angeles, where he later returned to lecture in the School of Engineering on the Teaching of Computer Systems.

Other contributions in research and information include papers presented at professional conferences, published articles in related fields, and membership in the distinguished, original Innovation Group.

Mr. Cosgrove is a member of the California Society of Professional Engineers, International Institute of Electrical and Electronics Engineers, Association for Computing Machinery, and the Data Processing Management Association. ∎

Software Protection for Computer Integrity and Privacy

. . . from an interview with Richard O'Connor

by Gion B. Green

Software that controls unauthorized access or accidental loss in a time-shared or multi-programmed computer environment . . . or through hardware or software failures. Vital considerations for a successful program discussed by a specialist.

In our enthusiasm for the computer we have jumped with great gusto into the twenty-first century. But in our jump we have in many cases forgotten the twentieth. Our anxiety to convert from ledgers or planning boards to computers has frequently led us to overlook some elements of the change we are undertaking. Among other things, many companies fail to notice that they are transferring valuable files from traditional company security to machines that are accessible to many people within the company or, in the case of time-sharing operations common with smaller companies, to many people outside the company, including competitors.

In a subject area as large as data security there are many lesser subjects, each of which can be discussed in depth. My primary areas of interest are control software that protect against erroneous or unauthorized distribution of data in a time-shared or multi-programmed computer environment; and control software that protects against accidental loss of data through hardware or software failures.

It is, of course, necessary to consider the computer system as a whole. Crucial to the continued operation of any system is an accurate and complete data source or data base. By 'data source' or 'data base' we refer to that basic information that is stored and accessible by computer at any given time. And it is this data base which must be protected to insure its content and structure at any time. The need for this protection becomes increasingly significant as we switch over to an ever-increasing reliance upon the computer. Unfortunately, security measures have not kept pace with this increased usage. Too many companies have simply assumed the safety of their files without having taken the relatively simple steps to insure that safety.

Let us examine some of the procedures that should be considered in insuring the integrity of computer programs. Our first step is to protect our data from loss through a mechanical malfunction. The simplest and most direct protection against loss is to duplicate all data. In other words, instead of the data base being recorded on one disc or tape, it is recorded on two through two different machines. This system permits separate storage of the tapes and it protects against hardware failure in that even if one of the machines suffers a breakdown, and we can count on that happening sometime, the other is still up and running.

There is, obviously, a cost factor in operating two machines simultaneously which must be taken into consideration. Businesses involving rapid, high-volume inventory change, airline reservations, or activities like International Reservations Corporation — one of our parent company's subsidiaries which deals primarily in hotel and automobile reservations — must have an immediate, up-to-date data base to handle random requests at any given time. With such applications it is usually desirable to have the protection of a second data base backup, even if there is extra expense involved.

It is possible to get very similar protection at less cost by simply duplicating any given material at any point after the information has been introduced into the computer. However, since the machine is out of service for other usage during the period when it is duplicating, this system is normally only used when the machine is operating in what is called a 'batch' mode. This means that the computer takes one job at a time, performs that job, and only then moves onto the next.

Today, however, machines also operate in the 'on-line' mode to accommodate a time-sharing system. This mode is one of the 'third generation' aspects. Computers have gone through three generations in their development; we're in the third generation now and will be in the fourth generation fairly soon. One aspect of the third generation machines is that mode where a computer can support many users simultaneously 'on-line,' with each of them interacting with the computer.

Since an 'on-line' mode implies multiple simultaneous usage of the machine, it would be intolerable to its many users to take it out of service to duplicate material even for a relatively short time. An alternate method is the creation of journal tapes containing 'before' and 'after' images of updated data base records. This technique permits a data base to return to its former status in case of a program failure of any kind simply by the application of all 'before' images to the on-line data base.

Through this use of journal tapes, a full and absolute data base regeneration in the case of a system failure can be performed. For example, if there is a failure in either hardware or software, the total data base duplicated at an earlier time can be restored to the on-line equipment. Naturally this restoration will be effected after the repair of the equipment or the software. This brings the data base up to date to some prior time period. This is when the 'after' journal tapes which were in process of creation after the duplication of the total data base — called a 'snapshot' — can then be applied to bring the data base up to a complete and accurate state just prior to the malfunction.

In either of these systems, or systems based upon the same concept, the securing of these stand-by or auxiliary tapes is of great importance. As with other physical assets of the company, it is essential that they be protected against loss, damage, theft or malicious mischief. When we think of the problems created by the destruction of a handful of company files, we can only shudder at the thought of the infinitely greater loss of only one computer tape.

Up to this point we have concerned ourselves essentially with the problem of data loss through breakdown. This is an issue which merits high-level thought and attention because of the operational and economic factors involved. However, a larger issue exists in any system where privacy or security of data is a requirement. Software techniques as well as hardware techniques and procedures must be created to protect against accidental or malicious dissemination of data to unauthorized personnel both within and without the company. Similar methods can be applied to computer systems, regardless of whether the need is for data privacy (in non-government applications) or data security (in government applications); so for our purposes we can think of them as identical problems.

An initial look indicates the need for protection of data files — regardless of whether they are on removable or non-removable storage media. Data may be stored on magnetic tape, which is easily transportable to a vault or other place of security; or on discs or cores which, in view of the fact that they weigh 10,000 pounds, may be considered for all practical purposes to be non-removable.

Basic security of this data is handled in third generation computer systems by a file system. A typical file system allows for the creation of a personal or unique file with the establishment of a password when the file is created. It is important to remember that the system must respond to the privacy of the password itself, and must prevent print- or readouts or system reviews that would reveal the password that provides access to a given file.

In addition to passwords, some files are further protected through a 'permissions' system. The names of valid system users can be explicitly stated to have certain very specific access to the file, such as *read, write, append only, execute only, etc.* In this way, a file can be put to its maximum use by allowing differing and restricted use simultaneously to various users at various levels of authority.

This last point cannot be overstressed. It is relatively simple to restrict an entire system to a few specially cleared employees. This approach, however, drastically restricts the potential of the technology at hand and probably hampers a sizable number of employees denied the machine who should have some access on a need-to-know basis.

Some years ago, sensitive information needed only to be protected at the computer itself; it was there that the information was produced in a paper printout. Now, to some degree, and certainly in the next ten years, thousands of companies will be operating on so-called management information systems. Often consoles, teletypes, remote devices, and the like will be located at various locations within the company building — or in several buildings net-worked by telephone lines across the country. Many of these stations will have the capacity to access the computer, from coast to coast or from one office to the next.

And since medium to small companies cannot afford their own large-scale computers, they will continue to deal with a service bureau on a time-share basis. The problem of privacy can be even more acute in this time-sharing situation, since certain sensitive information within the same computer has to be protected from competitors or from active industrial espionage.

The security of the location of the system user must always be considered when setting up a time-shared system with various station locations. A given user may have full authority to access certain information, but certain locations may be prohibited that data.

Remember, we are no longer dealing with a controlled location at the computer itself, with its discrete printout. Today's system, and the system of the future, includes multiple station installations, possibly with visual displays that may be viewed by numbers of unauthorized persons. Certain data must be denied to certain locations. As an example, the personnel manager is authorized to retrieve payroll information but not at any location outside the personnel department. If he were in some other part of the building and sought payroll information from some other station, the information would be denied him.

In order to control the release of data and prevent its falling into unauthorized hands, or being displayed in an unauthorized environment, a complete set of information detailing the authorities of each system user must be present within the computer system. Data release *qualities* must be associated with each remote output station. This information would relate the right of the individual to operate particular programs, and the limits, if any, of authority to retrieve specific data. Executive system controls must monitor each data access performed for a system user to insure that release of such data is authorized as to person and place.

Let's take one more look at a typical security environment that could appear to the on-line system user. The user would activate a remote station at which time he would be asked to declare his name, organization, and a private system password. The software could then identify the individual and verify his access authority, combine the result with the previously known status of the console environment and establish an access level for that person at that time at that remote station. The user could proceed by identifying the data bases in which he desires access, giving any further required passwords for such, and proceed with his task. At all times information retrieved for dissemination to this user could be validated against the established authority. If, at any point during the sign-on, sign-off, or on-line activity of the user, an attempt is made to access unauthorized data, the appropriate security alarm procedures must be initiated by the software.

One final note, which is, perhaps, the most critical element in the chain of data security: That is, of course, the personnel directly involved in programming. These people have specified and implemented the security controls. Certainly they know any weaknesses that may appear in these techniques. They could, if so motivated, skirt these security measures and obtain any data present in the computer system. Even if they are totally disinclined to inspect such data, they may be forced to 'dump' the system from time to time to correct problems that may appear.

A 'system dump' is trade jargon for an image of a computer memory taken at a given point in time. It's not all its devices, or necessarily all of its data base, or all of its information, but it is a copy of everything the computer is operating on at the moment. And it necessarily contains some data. If at that particular moment the computer was responding to three on-line users, a system dump has some of the data, at least, for three on-line users in the system. This information may or may not be private; it's purely a matter of chance what or how much information is revealed. But the possibility of revealing sensitive information to otherwise unauthorized personnel exists.

Therefore, in any privacy or security situation, certain people must be entrusted with access to any information contained in the system. Under these circumstances, appropriate background investigations to insure the integrity of the individual are warranted.

As an old industrial security motto says, "Security is everyone's business." Likewise, the assurance of privacy must be everyone's *concern*. ∎

THE DEEPER LOOK

PART 1

UNDERSTANDING THE PEOPLE WHO CONTROL YOUR COMPUTER'S SECURITY

Personnel is certainly the key to computer security. Beyond the protective software procedures, the best way to maintain computer security is for management to recognize those employees or contractors who are really in a position to do the company harm and take some steps to protect its assets from them. In the case of computer-related personnel such protection is not guards, access complexities, or identity validation, however. It is psychological.

One major step, for example, is to make sure that there is recognition within the organization for the properly higher status of the computer personnel group. As an elite group, they are personally aware of their contributions and like to feel that others know, too.

The frequent absence of this status in modern business has come about in a curious way. Historically, many computer operations within companies grew out of the accounting department. Because of this, a man who used to audit the bookkeeping now finds himself supervising the computer and establishing the organizational practices and job classifications that go with it. Hence, the status of people today being brought in to handle the computer on a professional level is still seen through the basic experience of the same man — and may not manifest any shift beyond the original job classification of the routine bookkeeper. Of course, this is not intended to put down the very important services of the bookkeeper! It is merely to underscore the extreme importance of making clear that the professional status of a computer programmer or maintenance technician is of a totally different magnitude.

The man who knows about the 'innards' of a computer and controls much of the company's destiny through his work with that machine is an entirely different breed of person from one who makes daily entries in a ledger.

Programmers run in extremes. A good one frequently works unbelievable hours. The time that he puts in may occur as overtime because he begins a program and can't afford to interrupt his thought process before its completion. Or, it may be necessary for him to be on the premises at a time when the computers are not being operated — so that he will not interfere with the normal ongoing process of business. But what he often finds is that he is only marginally excused for not always being at his desk from 9 to 5, in addition to the weekends and all-night sessions, and all the other time that he put in.

Because his supervisors are frequently not oriented to the nature of his work, they forget or are unaware that he has worked on Sunday for no overtime. The programmer finds himself called on the carpet because he was not at his desk during the daytime hours, or he came to the office at noon on certain days.

Part of this was a carryover from the accounting department orientation of the man who first became the computer supervisor by moving up through a very different route.

Part of it is that the organization is uncomfortable with the seemingly erratic computer personnel, even though he is actually doing part of his programmer's basic job in not keeping regular hours.

Management recognizes it intellectually. But frequently representatives of management and co-workers fail to recognize it emotionally, and this is a source of strain. In some instances, this gap in attitudes can lead to a very major crisis of confidence between computer personnel and management.

The potential for such a crisis of confidence represents a very real threat to the security of the computer and the company. The computer programmers who may be giving their all (but doing it in a way not recognized by, or parallel with, the standard corporate procedure set-up) have a tendency to develop resentment. *They* know that there are times when the greatest efficiency means working 48 hours straight, followed by complete collapse at home for a few days when nobody will see them. *They* know that they are most efficient when they become totally immersed in their latest assignment and then roll right through it.

So they find it an unexpected shock when they realize they have stirred a hornet's nest full of buzzing demands to "know where so-and-so has disappeared to." And if the time ever comes that even one such man is never seen again except when he picks up his final pay check, the corporate security battle may well be lost.

The computer men who are the best happen also to be the ones who are most sensitive to lack of appreciation by management and to the other proddings that cause normal human resentment.

The company that recognizes these factors, and makes provision for them to be handled adequately, has gone a long way toward guaranteeing the security of its computer. Properly treated computer personnel, who feel that they are duly respected and at least reasonably compensated, are far less inclined to 'prove something' to the company by compromising its computer, making a practical joke out of a program, or actually engaging in espionage for sheer satisfaction of their disgruntlement.

As we indicated earlier in this article, it is very important to know, if you are management, who it is that can do your company the most harm. Perhaps it is time to take a practical look at individual computer personnel, call them by name, and discuss the ways in which they can and might compromise a corporate computer operation from within.

Probably the easiest way to get at any computer is through the people who have authorized access to the area that you normally do not think of as having any kind of access at all. One of the first of these would be the fellow who has the broom and mop bucket in his hand and goes around in the area in the middle of the night. If the goal is genuine industrial espionage or malicious mischief, that man will be a Ph.D. in disguise and it won't take him long to get whatever he needs.

The next most obvious person is the computer maintenance repair man. Unlike a common, look-down-your-nose-at-him mechanic, these men are quite highly skilled; clearly they have to know the computer to be any good. They also have to know a fair amount about the operating system if they are going to function properly.

When we talk about security *vs.* criminal motive and opportunity, we must remember that computer maintenance repair men don't generally make a great deal of money. Also, they are almost always supplied by an outside source. Yet any one of those men can get to anything he wants in *your* company's computer.

The maintenance repair man is ostensibly under complete supervision of the computer operations supervisor. But generally they become buddies after awhile, and the operations man tends to consider 'his friend' above suspicion. In addition, the maintenance technician frequently has much more technical skill and information. The operations man probably could not keep track of what the maintenance technician is doing even if he made an energetic effort to do so.

As a normal part of his job the maintenance technician is flipping switches on that computer at a great rate! That switch-flipping is part of the way he does his work. Another person observing would have to be extraordinarily able to know whether he is doing just what he needs to do or whether he is extending himself beyond his area of privilege or responsibility.

In an effort to control this, certain effective but mindless procedures can be set up. For example, whenever the maintenance technician works on the computer the system disc, which contains the critical systems records, may be taken out of the computer or 'clobbered' (computer*eze* meaning the disc has received an overwrite, so that the maintenance technician has no way of getting at it).

However, such a procedure does not solve the problem of what happens when something is wrong with the disc itself. There is no way of escaping from the fact that some maintenance technician somewhere, at some time, must be allowed to get at that disc. You therefore are uncomfortably face-to-face with the fact that your system maintenance man is a primary source of concern, because he has a great deal of access.

The next man in line to be concerned about was just mentioned! He is the computer operations man. Typically these people work alone in the middle of the night at times like three o'clock in the morning, and on Sunday. Since the operations shifts go around the clock they are frequently very much isolated and can do anything they wish. To add to the problem, it is generally unavoidable that the lower grade people are the ones to be put on the night shift, because they are the only ones who will agree to it. In addition, there will be times when the computer is down completely during that shift.

Recognizing these complexities, it is possible to have certain procedures that make unauthorized access to the computer more difficult. For example, it is desirable to record all down time and to keep a chronological log that accounts for all the minutes. By forcing the lonely operations man to make logs, at least he has the responsibility of constructing a convincing lie to explain why an assigned task was not done, why the computer clock was reset, and so on.

By being able to review a log, the security-responsible parties at least have the possibility of spotting inconsistencies or irregular occurrences.

Unfortunately, however, there are ways around even that — because there are very common happenings that can cause the computer to go down. A simple power failure can cause 'a system crash.' If this happens, the cause of the 'system crash' is remedied, and then the operations man goes into restart procedures. The only answer he needs to give management for this gap is that something happened. Because 'something happens' all the time with complex machinery like computers, there are routine restart procedures and the exercise of these is not, and cannot be, considered suspect.

We are actually considering computer personnel in order of their dangerousness, and we have probably started at the bottom and worked up. What we have left is the systems programmer, who is conceivably the most dangerous of all. He has, by virtue of his job, the greatest degree of authorized access.

If the intent is criminal or malicious, and if the perpetrator is reduced to trying to obtain access 'by hook or crook,' certainly the maintenance technician can get the information. But it is not really part of his job to be making certain kinds of interrogations into the system, while it is routine for the systems programmer to make any kind of interrogation. Also, the systems programmer has that which the maintenance technician also does not have except by great stealth: he has the capability to modify the system.

A system contains hundreds of thousands of instructions that mean nothing except to very few persons who are extremely knowledgeable about particular details. The systems programmer can build in, and hide, a way of laying the system bare — available only to him. Remember that computer systems programmers have keen minds, which work in the fashion necessary to accomplish this kind of deception — and the ways that they build in of getting access for themselves are frequently ways that nobody else would be able to find.

This ability to modify a system for one's own purposes is probably the most powerful of any means of compromise. With that built-in access, the systems programmer has made it pos-sible to run very clandestine information dumps. He doesn't even have to run under a systems programmer number; he can 'palm it off' as just another job of cranking out an inventory summary or something equally ordinary.

It is probably worth pausing here to consider the personality of the systems programmer and its possible effect on security. On the whole, they have a little different way of looking at things and typically are more classically creative and artistic kinds of people. At the same time, they will be rather more easily offended by organizational rules — and the best of them are apt to be most offended of all. He certainly always has an acute sensitivity about his professional dignity. In many case histories of security breach, it is possible to find that a highly adept systems programmer has been given the merest slight, possibly only having management insist on the checking of his work by another man that he didn't think was competent.

Another thing to remember is that when the systems programmer quits there is no external way to keep him from carrying the very vitals of your operation with him. The fact that he does not do this depends solely on his loyalty toward you. And *that* is determined by your company's treatment of, and sensitivity toward, *his* personality and human needs.

It is extremely important that both security men and management recognize that the software men in their computer operation have the greatest capability of all for really compromising the basic 'innards' of their computer. Yet this is difficult within some companies. The security officer finds it hard to explain to the president that a bunch of men he has in an office somewhere near the basement, whom he makes punch a time clock, who are working for $200.00 a week or whatever, *actually have the ability to completely wipe out his company.*

In a very real sense, much of what we have just said about the systems programmer could apply to the computer operators also. And to the outside maintenance technician. And to the man who holds a broom in that section.

Since it is impossible to eliminate the opportunities, the only recourse and probably the best answer is to try to eliminate the reasons that might cause somebody to want to take advantage.

Security cannot be made perfect within a computer, because if you succeed in that you effectively prevent the door from being opened. And it is necessary to open the door to use the computer at all.

So, then, what else do you aim for? You see that necessary protections against human error and accidental compromise are implemented. Then you make sure that certain attitudes have been allowed for; you help management to recognize the importance of the genuinely critical people and beware of violating that.

SUMMARY

Remember that you are basically operating on percentages if yours is an industry that puts a great dependence on the computer. The greatest blow you can strike for computer security is probably in personal relations with your computer group. If they have a feeling of loyalty to the company, not only will they not engage in deliberate activities to compromise the computer, they will also be watchful and have a tendency to report anything suspicious so the company can spot trouble at its inception. The importance of this cannot be overstated, because it is astounding how easy it would be to slip past the attention of management.

Only in an operation where 'nobody seems to care' will you see the destructive whimsy of programmers and other computer personnel—who feel unappreciated and spiteful only because management has not yet properly awakened to the need to give them their just due! ■

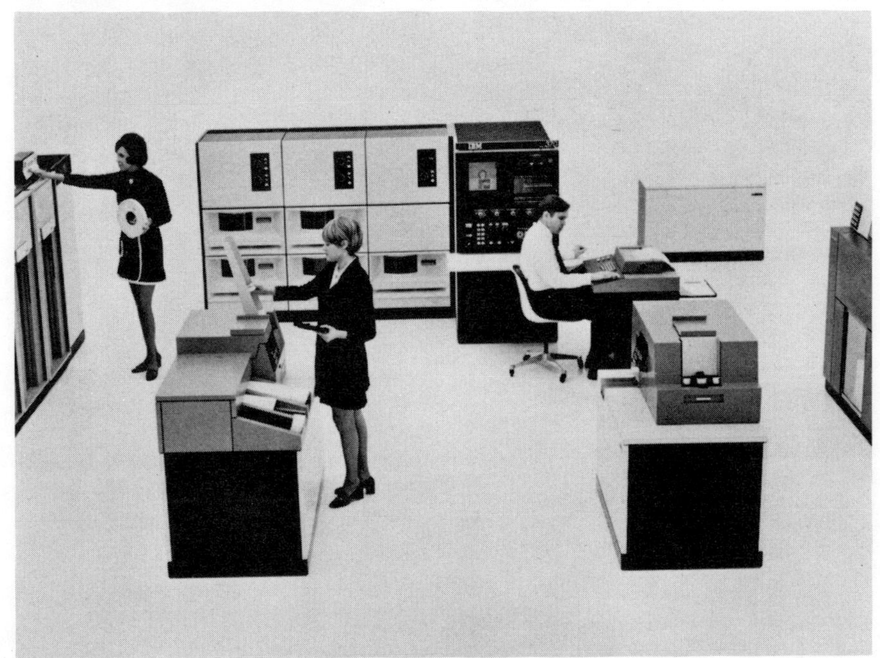

THE DEEPER LOOK

SO YOU THINK YOU WANT A THEFT-PROOF COMPUTER

The master executive may say, "Your number is good. I'll let you do these kinds of things." Or, depending on how the program exclusions are written, that master executive might say, "Your number is bad. You can't do these or these things that you are trying to do." Or, "You can't come into this system at all. I'm going to kick you off the system."

It's important to remember that all of this is done by the software and the numbers in the computer. The way in which the software is prepared, the way in which the numbers in the computer are lined up, and the instructions that their line-up conveys, is what does all of this.

The computer has no mind of its own. There has to be an individual (or several individuals) who writes that program, who instructs the computer through that program to do whatever he wants it to. There also has to be an individual who can make changes in existing programs, because all software systems are in a constant state of change.

The need to change a program can come from a variety of things. There may be new things that need to be added, or new things that cause a need for subtraction of certain specifications in the program. Or, someone finds an error in the output and an individual must go into the program and correct that error.

It is in the nature of computer systems that they are being constantly upgraded and modified. Human beings have the responsibility for doing the systems work and the programming in a computer installation.

For simple operations as, for example, somebody on the production line who needs an inventory, an application program is written. This program is built for the existing resources of the operating system and it causes the appropriate code numbers to bring up correct responses in the computer as wanted.

But if the application programmer finds that the program he is writing cannot be made to work on the existing system, he tells this to the more senior *systems* programmer. Then the systems programmer thinks about it and concludes that if he changes *a* and *b* and *c* it will then be possible for the application program to do *xyz* operation. In many installations he will then discuss it with his supervisor and the conclusion jointly will be to make a change to fit their need.

At this point the systems programmer will receive instructions to go and take care of changing the system. Mr. Systems Programmer then goes into the 'innards' of the computer system; he goes into what computer people call the source code and modifies that program; then he introduces that modified program into the 'master executive' that runs the computer day and night — the non-sleeping computer guardian.

The systems programmer does this relatively independently. It's likely that he is the only person who knows anything about what he has done, even though there may be two or three who cross-check each other to a certain degree.

The reality of the situation is that any given systems programmer usually comes back and says "Everything is working O.K., now. I've made this new system tape, and this is the one to use." Since there is no good reason to question, or no practical *way* to question really, it isn't long before that new system tape becomes the one that everyone uses.

Now, the security-responsible personnel must bear in mind, that new system tape *is* going to reflect whatever changes were agreed upon by the computer management. But it may *also* reflect any additional, unknown change that the systems programmer may have made, because nobody knows exactly what he has done. A certain amount of documentation of what is done is required, but it only reflects what the systems programmer says he changed; there is no way to verify or guard against those things that might be hidden inside.

As a matter of fact, it is rather rare that even the detail of the coding modification that implemented a particular change is documented. If a procedure were set up that required that, and if it were verified in each case, that would help maintain a secure computer.

Yet, like everything else that is under the control of man, there are ways around that, too. What you find is that the 'ways around' become infinite. There is a 'way around' everything that exists.

People frequently ask if there will ever be a time when the computer can be made espionage-proof or theft-proof. The only possible answer for that is: when and if such time comes, the computer will also become incapable of maintenance as well. And it will be incapable of change. It is impossible to permit access to the system or to the disc and still guarantee against espionage or theft.

Another way to answer that question is to say, yes, it is possible to make an operation theft-proof. After all, if nobody understands what's going on inside, there is no way that anyone can compromise that operation. But on the face of that answer it's obvious that as soon as you have made it theft-proof you have also made it effectively unusable.

One of the problems we face with computers now is that everyone who uses them does *not* have the knowledge of what goes on inside. And in that sense, things do tend to take on a life of their own; where people do not know what is going on inside they become victims of this machinery. The many clerks that service all kinds of nation-wide computer networks are constantly putting the man-on-the-street subscribers to a given service into this position. We are rife with jokes about ineffectual correspondence that is being carried on "with a computer."

In effect, the clerical persons and even the management persons responsible for the running of these large companies are not. deliberately trying to make it 'difficult' for the customers of, say, a credit card service, who develop problems because of computer errors or the inability to obtain proper information. They are, in fact, themselves victims of the machinery because they don't know what's going on inside the computer. And therefore they do not know how to translate the *real problem*, which has come to them by 'phone call or letter, into action within the computer.

The more theft-proof and espionage-proof a computer becomes, the more we are saying that the people using it, and using the products of it, neither know what is going on inside nor have a way of communicating with what is going on inside. So when you contemplate a totally theft-proof computer as some kind of ideal, what you are unknowingly asking for is to replace a chronic but controllable disease with a ' cure ' that would actually kill the patient. ■

INFORMATION – YOUR COMPANY'S GREATEST ASSET

By Thomas V. Sobczak, Ph.D.

One man's views on protecting information – the indispensable element that holds every company together, and without which it cannot function.

A new resource of strategic national and international importance has been developed. Some refer to it as information sciences, others as information process, and still others as communication.

The term employed in this report is information, one which, I think, is more embracing. The word is intended to mean the collection, storage, processing, dissemination, and use of information for profit. Further, it is intended to acknowledge the importance of man and the goals he has set for information technology, the values employed in making his choices, and the assessment criteria used to decide whether business is controlling the technology and is being enriched by it.

"Within two decades," says Max Ways, "these new information technologies have become an indispensable part of the web that holds society together. If it had to get along without these technologies, the business life of the United States would be imperiled to the point of disaster. The new ways of handling information have brought about fundamental changes—in government, industrial, and political processes. They have altered the psychological and cultural attitudes of hundreds of millions who have only the haziest notion of how the new technology works."

Today, information technology provides us with the capabilities for formulating and ordering our goals and priorities, from institutional to planetary; for increasing management's effectiveness; for freeing man to participate in broader and more meaningful activities and for narrowing, if not closing, the gap between the haves and the have-nots.

It is important to recognize its potential—for if we do not, we may drift in another direction. We may instead create and strengthen the power of management elites; circumscribe the freedom of man; and create a new kind of 'rich-poor' gap between those who, regardless of economic status, know how to command the information technology — and those who do not. Author.

29

In the American government, one speaks of *'Security'* in well-defined terms. There are, in fact, laws protecting both national security information and the proprietary information of the corporation.

However, in the world of the corporation there is less uniformity of meaning and less protection for the information being developed. This problem is referred to as the 'privacy problem'—*'privacy'* meaning *'isolation or freedom from unauthorized observation or modification of information'*.

Unfortunately, there is incentive to penetrate the privacy of industry. The information may be of significant value in providing embarrassing data to competitors in the business environment, or personal records may be wanted for malicious motives or profit.

Such penetration can be classified as the result of deliberate efforts to infiltrate the nation's information systems. However, 'accidental' disclosures —caused by equipment or people failures—are equally dangerous. A well-designed system in the business environment must protect against both types of privacy violations (deliberate or accidental) if information is to be protected.

If one thinks in terms of 'cloak-and-dagger' methods, the potential for deliberate penetration of a business to gain information is unlimited. Evidence of its truly great potential can be found in the many authors who have already commented in great detail on manual penetrations — *i.e.,* theft by stealth, physical break-ins, *etc.,* common to the business situation.

In this article, I have undertaken consideration of the penetration of a particular aspect—the business computer system. Consider a typical on-line computer system with remote terminals. 'Passive infiltration' may be accomplished by 'bugging' the telephone or inductively picking up information from a cathode ray tube.

Other possibilities include active infiltration by (1) a legitimate user accessing information from files he is not authorized to contact or (2) an unauthorized person using a legitimate user's device and code numbers.

The possibility also exists that unscrupulous computer programmers could deliberately leave 'weak' spots, thereby allowing unauthorized access; or maintenance men or operators could deliberately disable the screen of protection set up to require penetration for obtaining information. In each case, the potential for loss could become a reality.

This should be sufficient to awaken interest in the security privacy problem inherent in the computer, which is management's information bank. It is obvious that no matter how secure we make a computer system, someone can, given enough money, time, and effort, gain access. A good 'privacy' system, however, can make access so difficult that it discourages efforts to infiltrate for information. Further, a good system can record, and thus warn about, successful misuse.

In an inquiry system, bugging or passive threats are minor since they can only 'overhear' a small portion of the available information. They can't select the information they want, and they must accept the information that is processed during any given time period that they are in operation. An act of infiltration through a terminal, however, can divulge or modify important confidential information.

The significant privacy problems in the order of importance as we see them are:

(1) **Active infiltration**—via an on-line computer terminal for either misuse by a legitimate operator or masquerading by an unauthorized user.

(2) **Programming 'weak' spots —** either intentional or accidental.

(3) **Computer center security —** computer center being defined as the place where all information is resident on some type of random mass-storage device or on punched cards.

The following classes of protection can be used against these attempts to misuse data on the computer file:

(1) Access control passwords, authentication, and authorization.

(2) Processing restrictions, storage protection, and file access limitations.

(3) Threat-monitoring audits of requests for information, logbooks of all requests for information, and a computer-generated history of all information transactions.

(4) Integrity management — the combination of computer hardware programming, personnel, locks, and physical control of all devices within the computer center.

Although not all of these are applicable to all phases of information, nor do all phases of information require the same protection, this is a starting point for the design of a privacy system. To operate successfully, this privacy system should incorporate the following standards.

> **"Knowledge is of two kinds; we know a subject ourselves, or we know where we can find information upon it."**
> **—James Boswell***

*James Boswell, The Life of Johnson, Oxford University Press, London, 1965, p. 627.

First, physical control, or *location*, of the terminal is most important. Terminals should be in a secure environment and not subject to intrusion by random individuals. Guidelines should be established for handling of or access to confidential information.

Operating personnel must be considered as part of the control problem. The honesty of these individuals should be cleared to an appropriate level. All operators of the computer equipment should be subject to a common discipline and authority. There should be a supervisor on every shift who is fully informed regarding each individual's qualifications for access to private information, and the specifications of this operating doctrine must be considered a major part of the computer system's design for privacy.

The physical installation should be designed so that terminals are arranged in a manner that makes supervision as easy as possible. The problem of terminal control for devices located in customer facilities is even more difficult. One must impress on the customer the need for care in handling and protecting of information for his own security.

However, we cannot depend purely on physical location and security regulations to protect the computer installation. We must design privacy features into the system itself.

Thus, our second standard involves initial access control, or the attempt by a user to access information from the system. The most obvious method of providing for privacy is to require a multiple alphanumeric key to activate the terminal. By using the symbols available to the typical teletype unit, one can develop six million two hundred and fifty thousand possible combinations.

The access key should be changed periodically in order to keep it secure. The key must not be displayed on the terminal output device when entered.

This can be accomplished by using the full duplex code.

Failure to enter the proper key will deny the user access to the device, and the system will log (*i.e.*, print a hard copy record of) the attempted entry.

Thomas V. Sobczak, Ph.D.

Thomas V. Sobczak, Ph.D., is a Director, Information Processing for Waldes Kohinoor, Inc., Long Island City, N.Y., and a Systems Generalist whose interests cover the broad spectrum of information processing —from 'people' systems through automation systems.

He was awarded his Doctorate in Management at Sussex College, England, and completed graduate studies at Hofstra University, New York, and undergraduate work at St. John's University, New York.

Dr. Sobczak has been active in the dissemination of all phases of management information. He has published five books and 45 magazine articles, plus chapters in two compendia. He frequently lectures before university, business, professional, educational, and civic groups, and he has been awarded Certificates of Achievement by the AIIE, SES, AIM, AAM and AMA. He also contributes time as a lecturer for Nassau County and New York's Vocational Education and Extension Board.

Dr. Sobczak is a member of DPMA and AMA. He also is a committeeman on Production Forum, (Production Magazine); a fellow in the Institute of Directors, London; and Vice Chairman, New York Region, National Defense Executive Reserve, U.S. Department of Commerce.

Dr. Sobczak serves as advisor, on a part-time basis, to several large corporations.

Repeated failure to gain access should disconnect the terminal and print out a console message to the computer operator in the computer center for immediate attention.

Access keys should always be unique to each operator as an identification record to indicate who requested and looked at or modified the information. The use of individual entry code words is not difficult, yet it provides good protection.

At the end of the transmission, we reach our third standard, which would be a timed or manual shut-off of the terminal device. While the terminal is in use by an operator, there is no need to reverify the access key. When the operator leaves the terminal for any reason, however, it should be manually turned off by an instruction.

There is always the possibility that an operator will forget to do this. Therefore, it is desirable to have a timing mechanism that will disconnect the terminal from the file should the device not be used for a period of time. This can be done by the internal central processing unit clock within the computer and a short programming routine.

To reactivate the terminal to access information, the operator would then have to reenter his access key. This would prevent misuse in the operator's absence. The timing for an automatic shut-off, of course, has to be determined separately for each area of information in order to avoid too long or too short an access time.

The fourth standard or area of control is file access—*file* being defined as a universe of information that has particular import for the operation of the business.

Within the data base for a teleprocessing system, there is often information that is of a restricted nature that should not be accessed by arbitrary terminals. There are also systems that allow customers access to their own files, but to no others. In these cases care must be taken to insure the terminal integrity of the stored information—*i.e.*, against improper access.

The access key should contain codes that determine the admittance of a user to a particular file of information stored on a random mass-storage device. Restricted files should have a mechanism that requires special code keys to access. In some cases, it would be desirable to require a supervisor to enter these keys. A log can be kept of such entries to restricted or sensitive files.

Our fifth level concerns limitations on changes to information that can be made from a remote terminal. In many applications, terminals can be allowed to modify all stored information. However, this could provide an individual the opportunity to make an unauthorized change for personal benefit or malicious purposes. Once designed, systems should limit such modification to those fields that a terminal may properly change. In addition, all adjustments should be marked by terminal and operator.

In the case of an extremely sensitive information change, it might be desirable to have supervisory authorization required in the form of an additional key entered by an authorized official before the changes can be made. Terminals that are allowed no modification ability should be excluded by noting the access key. Attempts to modify information from such terminals should result in an instant 'shut off' of the terminal and a logging of the attempt.

The final degree of control is proper maintenance of the record of access to information. Maintaining of logs by the computer system provides a basis for threat monitoring to the privacy of stored information. These logs should be kept by the computer itself. Through such logs it is possible to detect attempts—both successful and unsuccessful—to violate security. The logs also help to locate the source of errors uncovered by audit.

Logs that should be kept include:

(1) Initial accesses that are attempted, valid and non-valid, with the time 'on' to the system and 'off' to the system.

(2) Sensitive files accessed.

(3) Modification to the information data base (what was and what is).

(4) Errors and improper requests from remote locations.

All logs should record the key word used for access and the records involved, thereby providing an indication of attempts to gain access. Successive improper entries from a terminal justify investigation. Large banks have specialized auditors to do this. The logs also can provide a checking mechanism for honest mistakes by operators in addition to the normal audit trail protection required in a reputable business.

One can safely assume that any programmer or analyst capable of designing and implementing a security system is capable of nullifying its intent. Aside from casting suspicion on the author, this remark is not intended to reflect on any particular individual —yet, it would seem wise to protect against the possibility of intentional or accidental intrusions via computer programming. The following procedures are suggested to minimize computer programming 'weak' spots:

(1) Program self-contained, defined modules separately by individual programmers with integration into the total program performed by a senior-type individual.

(2) Program access controls by an outside source or sources.

(3) Program for a supervisor's review display either in hard copy (*i.e.*, a computer typeout) or as a cathode ray tube (CRT) printout that requires additional keying to enter confidential files.

(4) Employ a subcontractor to evaluate and try to beat your system.

During implementation of a system, independent checks should be made of the privacy programs in order to eliminate accidental or deliberate weak spots.

It is a safe practice to implement each module separately, testing the modules before integrating, then testing the integration. Modifications in the form of patches must not be permitted. (*A patch is a minor change to an existing program without full documentation.*) A recompilation of the entire program should be made at each change.

When debugging of a module and its integration is complete, one should collect or destroy all copies of the master documentation. If kept, the master documentation should be stored in a highly secure place and made available only on a 'need-to-know' basis.

If modifications to the computer program are made or required after the privacy system is operational, these modifications should be treated as new programming and all the foregoing steps and controls adhered to. It is wise to disable files at such times in order to prevent accidental and unofficial access, and/or modification of data or damage to the records themselves during the program maintenance. If warranted, a switch-over to a dummy data file can be programmed; with that precaution, the off-hours activities can be traced and audited, and counter measures can be built-in to the privacy system to protect company information.

In addition to normal supervision, care must be taken to protect information stored on tape, discs, or data cells not tied into the on-line system because of alternate channel selection. (A condition wherein the physical hardware is not large enough to control all information files at one time.)

Personnel should be thoroughly screened and watched. A computer program librarian's loose lips can sink a high capital investment! And there is always the possibility of operator attempts at modification of information. In addition, a printout of stored data that contains private information could prove embarrassing.

Additionally, maintenance operations performed by a computer manufacturer's service or field engineering force open the door to the possibility of outside access to information in the system. A computer manufacturer should never be allowed to perform maintenance on hardware unless a representative of the lessee/owner is present.

In conclusion, the most successful approach to maintaining security for information in the computer center is a combination of supervision, operating procedures, and checks and controls of access to hardware. The problem of protecting removable files and backup tapes must be completely defined in operating instructions, and responsibility must be assigned for the 'hands on' control of removable tapes, discs, or data strips.

Finally, all output in hard copy form must be screened before it is removed from the computer center, and removal and distribution must be authorized, signed for, returned after use, and destroyed. ∎

ASSURED PRIVATE ENTRY:
One Man's Macro

By Thomas V. Sobczak, Ph.D.

A computer expert
shares with
SECURITY WORLD readers
his own overview of programming
instructions for protecting
your company's
computer-stored information...
with technical appendices.

As you will recall in Part I of this series, Information —Your Company's Greatest Asset, *we dealt with 'privacy' as related to unauthorized access to stored information at the corporate computer facility. In Part II we will discuss increasing loss of privacy to the* individual, *as 'personal' information becomes more and more computerized; and programming safeguards to combat this problem.—Ed.*

Part II

Privacy of information concerning the *individual* has become increasingly complicated to maintain as computer applications continue to grow.

Banks create central information files, industrial firms build personnel record files and customer account status, and government begins to tie it

Figure 1

Operator Failure Function (OFF)

Transfer from Checkpoint
Set Index Reg. 1 with Number of Terminals
Is Use Bit I on
No
Yes
Set TSB I Off
Set Use Bit I Off
Log Turn Off
Finished all Terminals
No
Yes
Decrease I by I
Return to Checkpoint

Assured Private Entry Macro

Transfer from LPS
Check 1st Char
key
Message
Type of key
Determine Source (Reg. 8) Add to header
turn
turn
Set TSB to OFF
Transfer to table for key check
Set source use bit ** on
Key Valid
No
Yes
Is TSB on
Yes
Was This 2nd error
No
Set ON in TSB
Set Proc. Byte to *YES
Yes
No
Request proper key
Console Message of Error
Set error count in TSB
Log with Date & Source & Time
Return to LPS Process or NO Process

*See Appendix 2 for description
**Optional for "OFF" See Appendix 4
- Optional if logged elsewhere

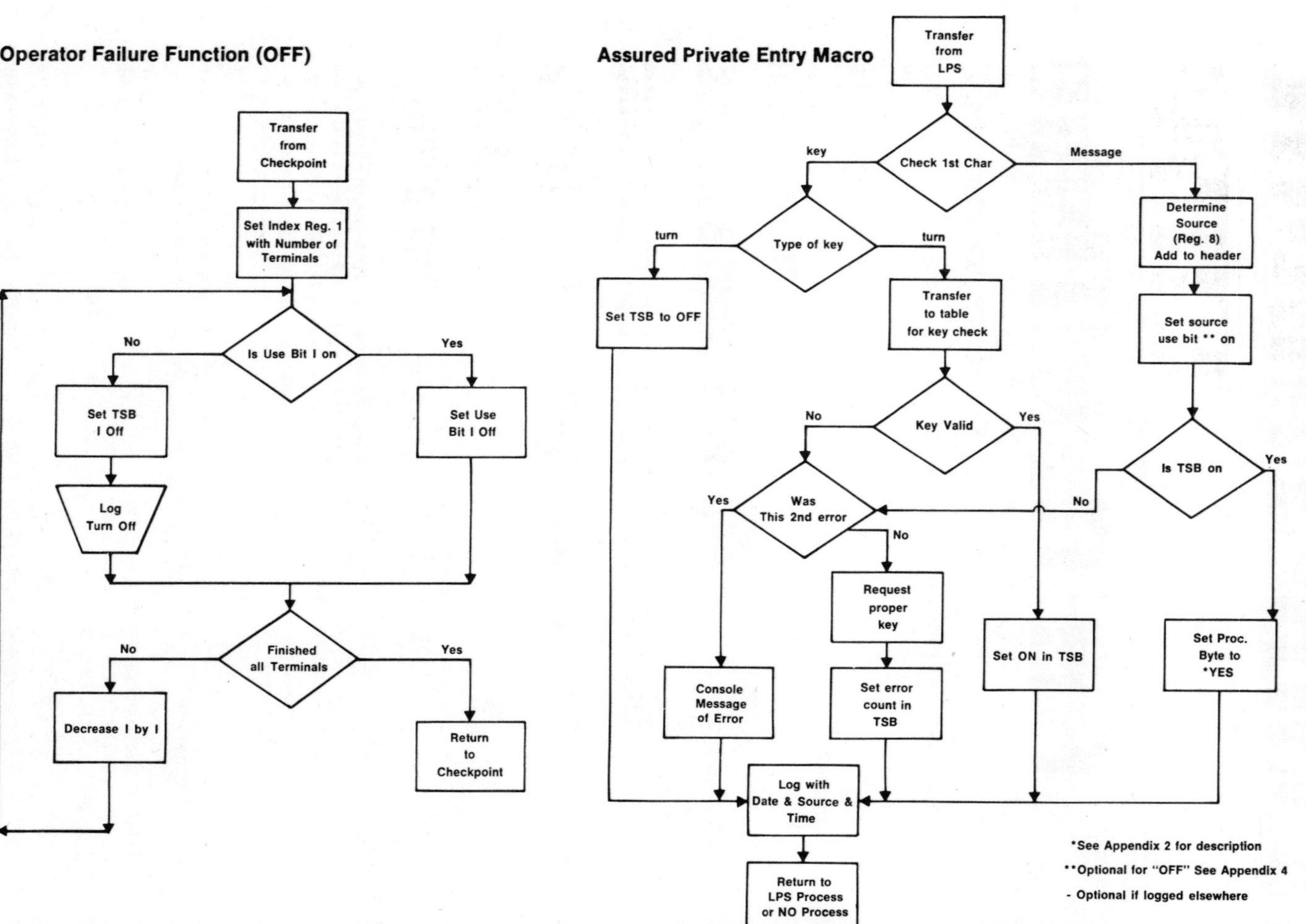

together with social security number identifiers. The foregoing only begins to scratch the surface of yet unmeasured icebergs called *information technology.*

One solution to the magnitude of the problem is to define a system of assured private entry for on-line privacy of computer-stored information.

I have developed the ASSURED PRIVATE ENTRY *macro,* a basic component of a 'model' security system. (A *macro* being defined as an overview of many programming instructions created to minimize the amount of detail presented in this explanation.)

In order to operate the terminal the operator must enter a code that the ASSURED PRIVATE ENTRY *macro* verifies before activating the terminal. The ASSURED PRIVATE ENTRY *macro* logs the code key, the terminal number, and the time of access. Neglect or failure to properly access causes a message to be printed on the console typewriter, alerting the computer operator at the central data processing facility for appropriate action.

Code keys should consist of some unique symbol not used in the inquiry, such as the '$' followed by an alphanumeric combination that is changed monthly. Terminals or remote-access devices should have a unique code key, so that the logging will keep a record of who used the terminal and which terminal was used. Following the entry of a key code the terminal security 'byte' (TSB) is set to 'on', and the terminal may then go on-line to the information file desired.

As each message is entered the ASSURED PRIVATE ENTRY *macro* verifies that the TSB is on and adds a code number to the head of the message identifying the source terminal. Use of time standard and log segment computer subroutines also can be added to cause a message to be kept on tape or a computer hard copy (printout) with the date, time, and source terminal listed.

From this point the message is processed in the usual fashion. A manual terminal 'turn-off' similar to the 'turn-on' above should be provided. The ASSURED PRIVATE ENTRY system is described more fully in Appendices 2 and 3.

An additional feature that is desirable is an automatic 'shut-down' or 'operator failure' function (OFF). This causes the terminal to be shut down if it is not used for a specific period of time. To restart the terminal the operator has to reenter the code key. The OFF feature provides protection when the operator forgets to manually shut down the terminal. OFF may not be needed for all projects, thus is not required in the ASSURED PRIVATE ENTRY system, but could easily be added to it.

Appendix 4 describes the implementation procedure. ASSURED PRIVATE ENTRY is a basic step toward an access privacy system; it can be modified to fit future privacy needs.

One feature that could be desirable in future systems would be the ability to partition the information to be accessed into several 'restrict access' groups defined by the information contained in them.

This could be done by using the *access code* key to identify the information groups that may be entered. The operator would enter the key and set the TSB to 'on' for the particular information group to be accessed. For each message the ASSURED PRIVATE ENTRY safeguard would check the TSB to determine the validity of the request and log it for reference. Special keys for specific files could be set up.

The question should be asked, *"What does this particular system buy in security and what does it cost?"* — ASSURED PRIVATE ENTRY 'buys' entry control in the form of a key that limits use to authorized operators. Far more important is the logging of *who* did *what.* This makes it possible to detect

Figure 2

Summary of Countermeasures To Threats To Privacy And Security

Countermeasure Threat	Pass Word	Logging & Audit	File Partition	"Off"
Browsing or Snooping	Good if pass word changed often enough	Identifies attempts at records source	Limits range of snooping	Protects if operator absent
Masquerading as Legitimate User with Code Key	No protection	Records source for post facto action	Limits range to that of user being imitated	Protects if operator absent
Theft & Fraud	Limits to Authorized Persons	Records for post facto action	Limits attempts to certain areas	Limits to authorized persons in operator's absence
Errors	Not applicable	Records source and records for post facto correction	Limits range of mistakes	Not applicable
System Failure	Not applicable	Provides records for recovery of updates	None	None

* No protection offered on following:

Wire tap / or bugging / Wastebasket or paper records / 'Trap Doors' or entry by system personnel.

improper use and to further identify the *individual* responsible. In a computer environment ASSURED PRIVATE ENTRY is a policeman guarding against theft as no manual supervisor could.

The second part of the question, relating to cost, is somewhat more difficult to estimate. There are no timing figures that any computer manufacturer will put in writing.

An estimate has been made employing the assembly language execution time for a well-known computer. It would seem that for a project of six hours the central processing unit overhead for privacy would amount to about two minutes per day. Although this is very definitely not a firm figure, it does indicate that the cost is not expensive.

Terminal time is minimum, amounting to just a few seconds to enter the code key in the morning and after shutdowns. The printer time involved in generating a log depends on the volume of transactions. Man-hours must also be allocated for reading this log. After initial 100% checking, spot checking will suffice.

In designing privacy systems for projects it is important to remember the need to tailor the protection to the requirements of the particular project. With ASSURED PRIVATE ENTRY, any one of the various parts can be set up independently. Thus protection can be designed to specific requirements. A summary of the protection provided is shown in the chart: *Summary of Countermeasures to Threats to Privacy and Security.*

BIBLIOGRAPHY

1. **Auerbach Communications Terminal Digest,** Auerbach Corporation, Philadelphia, Pennsylvania, 1971
2. **Auerbach on Time Sharing** (Computer Technology State-of-the-Art Series), Auerbach Corporation, Philadelphia, Pennsylvania, 1970
3. **B-3 Operating System Manual,** National Cash Register Company, Dayton, Ohio, 1969
4. **Control Through Information, A Report on Management Information Systems,** American Management Association, New York City, New York, 1963
5. **Information Technology, Some Critical Implications for Decision Makers,** The National Industrial Conference Board, New York City, New York, 1972
6. **Introduction to Century Hardware and Software,** National Cash Register Company, Dayton, Ohio, 1967
7. **SAFE: Security Audit and Field Evaluation for Computer Facilities and Information Systems,** Firebrand, Krauss & Co., East Brunswick, New Jersey, 1972
8. **Scientific American** (Information Issue), Scientific American Incorporated, New York City, New York, September 1966

APPENDIX I

Abbreviations and Definitions:

APE	**Assured Private Entry** — the proposed set of assembly language instructions to carry out the basic security checking and logging. This is user-written **macro,** not supplied by any computer manufacturer.
TSB	**Terminal Security Byte** — a byte for each terminal set to 'on', 'off', or 'failure' representing the terminal status with regard to security. The failure status is entered in the byte if the wrong security key is entered.
LOGSEG	Manufacturer-provided **macro** to copy incoming messages to peripheral unit.
LPS	**Line Procedure Specifications** — portion of an operating system that specifies the procedure for handling incoming and outgoing messages.
OFF	**Operator Failure Function** — feature to be user-written as part of APE.
Checkpoint Restart:	A manufacturer-provided utility program to save certain records periodically as a protection against failure. Should difficulty occur, it is then possible to resume processing from the last checkpoint.

APPENDIX 2

System Design:

Flow Chart I is in the form of an assembly language user sub-routine or **macro.** Local modifications to this design can be made for the various uses.

Potential modifications include:

1. **Logging** — if the incoming messages are logged elsewhere in the system no log procedures are required in **APE**.

2. **Timestamp** — optional if the incoming time is desired on messages.

3. **Header Arrangement** — the order in which Timestamp, etc., appear within the header. This is more or less a matter of taste.

Flow Chart I has a note referring to a processing 'byte'. This is included in the header to indicate to the message-processing program whether it should process the message or not. Code keys and improper messages require no processing beyond **APE**. Other messages, such as an inquiry, do require processing. One byte is reserved in the header to indicate this. A sample header, subject to the modifications previously mentioned, is shown below. The precise arrangement is, of course, variable.

Processing Byte	Source Terminal	Number (Variable)			Time	Stamp	(Variable)			Messages	
1	2	3	4	5	6	7	8	9	10	11	'''
1	0	2	7	b	1	1		4	6	Messages	

A separate program to update the privacy program by changing the key word is included in **Appendix 3**. In addition, a tape-to-print or disc-to-print program is required to print out the log.

APPENDIX 3

Modifying the Code Key Word:

In the flow chart of **APE** a transfer to the key table is shown. This is done to make that table independent of the system and, thus, easy to change. The code key is flexible and may be used only for identification or for security as well. Code keys should be changed periodically if they are to be useful for security. The specific method to accomplish this is debatable. So far, two possible suggestions have been developed. These are summarized below. It is difficult to say which is best for any particular application. Probably the decision should be left to the person implementing the security section of the program.

1. **Data Set** — establish the code key as a separate data set with a program to update.

2. **Supervisory Terminal** — establish a supervisory terminal with the ability to modify the code key segment.

APPENDIX 4

Operator Failure Function (OFF)

The **OFF** is a user-written option that may be added to APE to automatically turn off the terminal when it is not in use. The inclusion of this system as part of the privacy design may not be necessary for all projects, thus the independent construction. In planning privacy, this programming function should be considered and implemented as needed.

In the basic flow chart **(APE), Appendix 2,** there is provision for a use bit for each terminal, which is set on whenever that terminal sends a message. This means setting up enough bits, one for each terminal, and putting a "1" in that bit whenever there is a message sent.

A sample is shown below:

Terminal #	1	2	3	4	5	6	
	0	1	0	0	1	1	

OFF checks these bits periodically to see if the terminal has been used since the last check. If it finds a "1", indicating use, it resets the bit to "0" and goes on. On finding a "0", indicating no use, it turns off the terminal and logs the action (see **Flow Chart 2**).

OFF is embedded in the Checkpoint Restart service modules. This provides the timing function of checking about every 15 minutes. This also keeps the **OFF** in the same module as poling thus avoiding inter-partition problems. It should be placed in the available space of modules not needed by poling requirements or in a separate additional module. The latter arrangement provides flexibility should revised releases of modules be significantly longer.

Partitioned Files

In many applications it may be desirable to split files into various sections and then control access by section rather than to allow general use. Various methods for achieving this partitioning of files are described below.

1. **Key on Each Message** — This would involve requiring the input generator to enter a code key on each message accessing certain files. This would be appropriate for files containing restricted information that is seldom required. It would seem an appropriate control for management reports and other documents of a sensitive nature that might be wanted on a daily basis only. Implementation would involve placing a checking routine in the user-implemented, message-processing program. This would be in addition to the **APE** described in **Appendix 2.**

2. **Partitioning by Terminal** — As an alternative to requiring the operator to enter a code key on each transaction, the system can be arranged to allow each terminal to have access to different restricted sets of files. This arrangement is in addition to the other parts of **APE,** which should also be a part of this system. The user-written, message-processing program must be written so it will check the source terminal identification placed in the header by **APE.** The access to certain files is then determined by a table based on the source terminal code. This table does not change frequently since terminals are effectively dedicated to certain use. Protection against use of terminals by unauthorized persons is still provided by **APE.** The partitioning is further limitation. This ties in closely with the idea of a supervisory terminal approach which would seem desirable.

Embezzlement by Computer

by Alan Adelson

**Employees can program computers
to steal for them, and then remove
the instruction, leaving no evidence.**

"I could steal a company blind in three months and leave its books looking balanced," boasts Sheldon Dansiger, a burly, 33-year-old data processing specialist.

His methods: Electronic embezzlement. His accomplice: The company's own computer.

Increasingly, business transactions that formerly were recorded on ledger pages are being translated into magnetic impulses in a computer's memory section. It's a simple matter for a crook with technical know-how and a little imagination to program a computer to fleece a company and fool its auditors, according to Mr. Dansiger.

He says corporate executives rarely question the reliability of financial results that emerge from complex million-dollar machines. "They simply forget that the machines have been built to do whatever the operators direct," explains Mr. Dansiger. "There's nothing to stop them from working quite efficiently for a crook."

MISSING MONEY

Joseph J. Wasserman, who heads a Bell Telephone Laboratories task force seeking to devise methods of auditing computers used by the Bell System, says many companies already have been hit with heavy losses, but their managements don't know it. He predicts that within a few years someone will uncover a computerized embezzlement that will make even the $150-million salad oil swindle seem puny.

Computers are operating faster and faster and producing fewer and fewer of the printouts that auditors and financial officers need to follow the flow of dollars processed by the machines. "If auditing staffs don't get involved in designing computer systems soon, they might as well climb up on their stools, pull down their green eyeshades and pray for retirement to come," says Mr. Wasserman.

Others who are aware of the growing problem echo the sentiments of Messrs. Dansiger and Wasserman. "If I were a crook, I'd work through computers," asserts Robert Fano, a leading computer theoretician at Massachusetts Institute of Technology. Ralph Salerno, a former New York City detective who is now a member of a state committee investigating organized crime in New York says: "I'm not a gambling man, but if I were, I'd bet a month's pay that the Mafia will be working with computers in a few years."

BILKING A BROKER

A number of electronic embezzlements already have come to light. The manager in charge of back-office operations at Walston & Co., a New York brokerage firm, electronically siphoned $250,000 out of the company between 1951 and 1959. By the time the theft was uncovered, the man had become a vice president.

He programmed Walston's computer to transfer money from a company account to two customers' accounts — his and his wife's. The computer was further programmed to show the money had gone to purchase stock for the two accounts. Then he sold the stock supposedly purchased, pocketed the cash and transferred some more.

When a Walston official sensed something was amiss, an examination of the two accounts revealed major irregularities. But the company could not figure out the embezzler's system. Because he hadn't stolen any money from customers' accounts, "what he did was absolutely undetectable without internal auditing," says William D. Fleming, Walston president. "Before it happened no one dreamed such a thing was possible, and if he hadn't explained how he did it, we probably still wouldn't know."

The thief explained to Walston's incredulous directors that he pulled off the elaborate money swap by going into the office early Sunday mornings to punch new computer cards and feed them into the machines. "It took someone with absolute knowledge of the computer system to do it," says Mr. Fleming. "This guy was the boss back there. He set up the system and ran the whole show."

"ANYONE COULD DO IT"

Walston recovered only a fraction of the stolen money. The firm promptly revamped its computer system, instituting a quarterly internal audit and other safeguards designed to foil embezzlement attempts. The former vice president served a year in Sing Sing prison and is now a furniture salesman.

Even as the Walston theft was being uncovered, a similar embezzlement was beginning at another New York brokerage firm, Carlisle & Jacquelin. From 1959 to 1963, the firm's data processing manager got away with $81,120 by instructing a computer to write checks to fictitious persons and send them to his home address. The scheme was uncovered when the Post Office accidentally returned one of the checks to the firm and the clerk who received it became suspicious.

George Muller, a managing partner of Carlisle & Jacquelin, refused to discuss the case. "We'd have to be crazy to give out all the details now so that anyone who wanted to could do it again," says Mr. Muller. Court records show that the embezzler was convicted, returned the money and received a suspended sentence.

More recently, National City Bank of Minneapolis discovered that the employee programming the computerized check-handling system it set up in 1965 embezzled $1,357 over a period of about a year. He programmed the computer to completely disregard his personal checks any time his account had insufficient funds to cover them. The computer allowed each of his bad checks to clear the bank and didn't debit the employee's account for the overdrafts.

The scheme was discovered only by accident, when a computer breakdown forced hand-processing of some checks. One of the embezzler's bad checks bounced. When bank officials confronted him, the employee readily disclosed his scheme. The ex-employee later pleaded guilty, repaid the money and received a suspended sentence.

Computer specialists tell of other ways employees can program computers to steal for them. A crook can change one figure in a computer program, and the machine will report abnormally high inventory losses as normal merchandise breakage, enabling accomplices to steal vast amounts of goods from warehouses without the theft being noticed. Later the operator can remove the evidence simply by putting the original figure back into the computer program.

Computerized payroll systems are potential bonanzas for embezzlers, the experts say. A computer operator can create paychecks for fictitious employees and pay extra overtime and wages to himself quite simply.* If he's more ambitious, he can program the computer to deduct a few extra pennies of "income tax" from every paycheck in the plant and pay himself the amount collected.

UNSAFE SAFEGUARDS

It's possible to program some safeguards against embezzlement into computers, the specialists say, but the process is complicated and costly and sometimes involves entirely rewriting computer programs and shutting down the machines for a time. Adding safeguards "will cost a company money, and the temptation is often to economize," says Roy Freed, counsel for the computer control division of Honeywell, Inc.

But even the most elaborate safeguards might not foil a skilled embezzler. There's always the danger that a crook will come along who's more clever than the specialists who programmed the safeguards into the computer. Lloyd McChesney, chief examiner for the New York Stock Exchange, says that although member firms recently tightened their computer auditing procedures, "no one has yet developed a way to keep his books with a 100% guarantee against embezzlements."

Data processing specialists, however, say there are a few basic rules company officials can follow at least

---

Even simpler was the method of a Los Angeles county employee in the data processing section, who simply held the 'repeat' button down when his own pay warranty was being printed, and set out to cash 200 identical, valid warrants. He had cashed about 30 when he was apprehended. — Ed.

to make it more difficult for a computer crook to raid the corporate treasury.

A cardinal rule, according to the specialists: Don't let the computer programmer actually operate the machine. A crook who can build a loophole into the system and also feed it the data necessary to carry out his embezzlement scheme is more likely to succeed than a crook who, after programming the machine, must sit back and hope another operator will innocently let the machine divert funds to him.

COMPUTER SLEUTHING

Manuel Stonewood — who, with Mr. Dansiger, operates a New York management consulting and "computer sleuthing" firm called EDP Associates Inc. — says he passed up some golden opportunities to steal large sums from a major New York City bank not long ago. "I alone designed a mutual fund's dividend system for the bank, wrote the program for it, then ran the job on the computer," says Mr. Stonewood.

"The operation was so big it had a mistake tolerance of several hundred thousand dollars," claims Mr. Stonewood. "I could have paid at least half that much to myself in small checks if I had been so inclined, and the money wouldn't have been missed."

A second rule recommended by the specialists: Segregate computerized check-writing operations from the departments that authorize checks. This setup makes it difficult for an embezzler to convert fudged data into actual cash pay-outs. And it makes it easier for management to spot checks issued by a computer that has been tampered with.

Another rule: Transfer computer programmers and operators frequently to different machines and different programs. The theory is that if a crook knows he won't be working on a single job long enough to bilk it for large sums, he's less likely to go to the trouble of rigging the computer to steal. Even if he does rig it, the next man on that job may spot the embezzlement procedure.

PHONY FACILITIES

What such safeguards fail to prevent, auditors are supposed to catch, of course. But many data processing specialists say most auditors don't understand computers, so a clever embezzler can fool them. Some large accounting firms have developed their own highly skilled staffs of computer auditors, but even these specialists can be deceived because so much of what goes on inside the machine never appears on a computer print-out.

"Unless you built right into the system a means of printing out audit information, you aren't going to get readable financial records anymore," says Mr. Wasserman of Bell Labs. He says his team of specialists already has developed several new computer auditing techniques that might eventually be used throughout the Bell System.

One technique involves programming a computer to spot seeming irregularities in operating procedures and immediately print out a copy of the questionable transaction for auditors to examine. Another method involves feeding test data into the computer and then checking to determine whether anything interfered with proper processing.

Mr. Wasserman says the Bell System's auditing setup will do far more than spot crooks. For one thing, it will alert executives more quickly to fluctuations in overtime costs, inventory changes and other areas that can have an immediate impact on corporate profits. He says computers currently are used to check the efficiency of telephone operators and to audit employes' calls to guard against widespread misuse of long-distance equipment.

TAPS TO STEAL COMPUTER DATA: HOW FEASIBLE?

What are the microwave links, the dedicated land lines, and the ordinary telephone lines giving to the computer data thief? Are these transmission vehicles providing easy access to all of our corporate secrets?

Because computer access on shared time arrangements is frequently obtained by dedicated land lines or by means of telephone lines, a great deal has been written lately about the possibilities of computer pilferage through tapping either of these phone lines enroute, or placing taps on egress lines leaving the company offices for the underground cable. In addition, awed sounds are being made about the possibilities of compromising computers through a microwave tap.

SECURITY WORLD went out looking for some computer experts, and asked them some pointed questions about the real security problems involved in potential tapping of all kinds. As a result, in the following article, various kinds of taps are defined and their possible percentages of danger are evaluated.

TELEPHONE TAPS

A standard telephone tap is understood by security officer and layman alike. Whether that tap is planned for a regular telephone line or on a dedicated land line, the electronics and procedures for tapping would be the same. The protection instituted to safeguard the computer transmission against such a tap would have to be the same as that instituted to protect a normal voice—though there is greater danger of losing accuracy in transmission with computer data.

However, it is probable that scrambling is not really necessary in the case of computer data transmission if it goes out as encoded information. Several factors actually mitigate in favor of the privacy of such a transmission. First, the computer transmission is digital, not analog, as is the voice. Second, it is structured according to the program of the system *into which* the information is being fed, and *from which* the information is coming.

In order to decode such information, that is, to make the information usable to anyone tapping the lines to steal the transmitted sounds, a great deal of expensive talent and equipment would be required. Finding the proper lines would itself be an enormous task once the transmission had gone onto multiplex cable. Beyond that, it would take time—and the use of talent and equipment cited above—to break the code.

While it might be worthwhile in certain cases of industrial espionage to invest the money for talent and equipment to steal the information by tapping, the percentages are against satisfactory or rewarding results because of *time*. That is, by the time the tap is accomplished, replayed for experts and machines, and puzzled over until the code is broken, that information would probably no longer have any *timely usefulness*.

The very real problem mentioned above of finding the proper transmission when tapping into telephone lines or dedicated land lines should also be considered a factor in favor of security. Literally hundreds and even thousands of transmissions are carried over any one given cable at one time.

Clearly the problem of isolating the stream of sound needed to complete the tap would be at best challenging.

A MICROWAVE LINK

In certain instances, something called a microwave link is used in the telephone transmission system. It can be described as "just another way of running a wire, except that it does not happen to be a physical wire."

What happens is that the material carried on the telephone lines up to the point where the microwave link begins is then transmitted by waves through the atmosphere across a particular area and picked up at the scheduled reception point (where the microwave link ends) to be put back on the telephone line and continued on its way.

If, for example, the telephone lines are being run through mountainous country, it is much easier to send from peak to peak than to lay lines overland. A small transmission station may be built on one knoll, and another station built 40 miles away on another knoll. Each would have two small antennas that would point at each other and be able to send messages directly across the gap instead of running down and around over hundreds of miles of rough and rugged land where it would be difficult to properly lay the cable.

The beam of transmission for microwave is fairly narrow. However, it is possible to actually set up equipment a half-mile away and pick up enough of the stray energy to record what is happening. Again, of course, such a pickup would be a terribly expensive proposition; and, again, once the data is acquired it still has to be turned into something usable.

Further, setting up equipment complex enough to complete the total theft operation might be difficult to do undetected. But it is possible to set up a small installation to record the microwave information so that the thief can take it somewhere else to work on it. Such a tapping would use video recording to put the microwave on the tape.

The microwave link can be thought of as nothing more than a two-way television transmitter, and we would be talking about picking up the voice (audio) portion only if we were tapping a microwave link.* Microwave transmissions can only be accomplished on a line-of-sight basis. There is no infiltration of alien transmissions from unexpected geographic areas such as occur with an AM radio.

HOW DOES WAVE TRANSMISSION WORK?

Consider a radio wave, which you can think of as pure tone, at a million cycles per second. (Compare this mentally with a high frequency note on the piano which may be ten thousand cycles per second in order to get a clear idea of what we are talking about.) The frequency is a million cycles, then, compared to the ten thousand cycles of a high piano note.

Next, the wave is electronic. It is a wave on which you can impose something called modulation. If it is amplitude modulation, that means the person transmitting can make the *amplitude* of the modulation bigger or smaller at the rate of the information he wants to transmit. For amplitude modulation, then, you have a basic wave frequency and you have superimposed information on that wave in modulated, overriding waves of controllable amplitudes. Remember the amplitudes are made bigger or smaller depending on the amount of information that has to be transmitted.

Within a small range, it is also possible to change the *frequency* of the

---

carrier wave (or band). This is called frequency modulation. If instead of a million cycles per second you make it just a few cycles below or a few cycles above, you can change back and forth. This gives additional flexibility.

Now, if you accomplish this preparation of the carrier wave and the overriding modulation in microwave, it is possible to transmit it with a very small antenna and also focus it in a tight little beam, so that with relatively low power you can get good quality transmission to another precise point.

As a matter of fact, the precision is so great that if you are just a few degrees off target the beam won't be received at all. That is one of its advantages; the transmitter can focus directly on the target instead of wasting a lot of energy splashing the transmitting information all over the side of the mountain! This type of transmission has been analogized as "focusing the sunlight to burn out the little ant." The convenience factor of using this method is great. That is the reason for overlaying modulation on carriers to transmit over space on what is called a microwave link.

TAPPING MICROWAVE LINKS

First of all, it is necessary to have a receiving antenna on your secret interception that will pick up a microwave out of the air. From there on you have a choice.

Your first option is to record it undetected. If this is done, you have not demodulated the information that you have imprinted on the magnetic video tape. You have not removed the carrier in order to isolate the modulation. You have merely recorded directly all that has been transmitted. Typically, that takes a higher level of recording capacity because a microwave is very high frequency.

Another alternative is to attempt to have some detection circuits in the equipment, and then record the detected material rather than the total transmission. There would be less of a problem in the recording process, but it is also very likely that you would lose some information as you were tapping because the detection method may not be exactly the same as the modulation method used in transmission.

What we are really saying is that some recordings that try to detect before they record may encounter modulation that is hard to untangle and therefore miss some of the data. There are ways of modulating so that it makes it difficult for somebody who doesn't know exactly what your techniques are.

There is nothing magic about the microwave link. It is certainly harder to tap into than a telephone line in that it is probably more expensive to do so. On the other side, it may be a bit easier to do the tapping undetected. Also, microwave links typically carry thousands of channels. So the problem immediately becomes one of which channel is the one you want, and how do you isolate it?

SUMMARY

Certainly theft of information by tapping either telephone lines or microwave links is technically *possible*. However, despite all-too-rampant scare comments about such taps as a large threat to the security of computer information, the security officer should take more careful stock. Considering the time-factor, the complexity and the cost, there is every reason to feel that, if such a tap were executed, the stakes would have to be so high as to be perhaps at the level of separate governments, and the financial resources on a par.

Perhaps one day these elaborate taps will be a proper concern to the security officer. In the opinion of those we talked with, however, the time for concern at this level is not now. ■ **49**

COMPUTER THEFT BY COMPUTER

By William Godbout

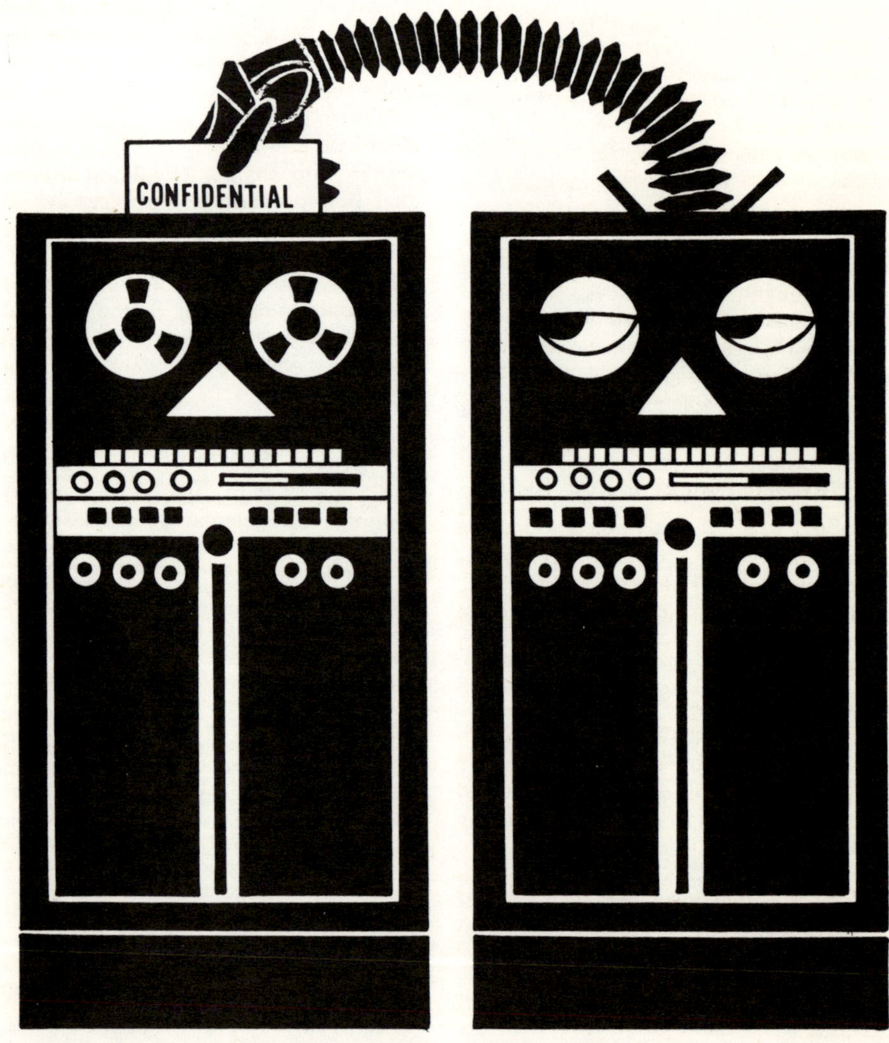

THE RECENT West Coast " 'theft' by computer from a computer" deserves careful and accurate reporting, because it represents what must be the first publishable breach of this type—the "theft" or, more accurately, unauthorized acquisition of information by a computer from a computer. It is important to recognize that no unique or unknown method was involved; the risk by which the loss occurred was a known possibility believed to be widely improbable in a commercial application.[1] In fact, the response of a computer utility executive to a direct question tells the whole story: "Yes, we could access [another company's] computer, of course — but it just isn't *done*." Now that it has been done, however, computer utility management is having to give a hard look at risks which may be unlikely or "unsportsmanlike," but can occur.

The complainant and plaintiff in the California case is Information Systems Design, Inc., an Oakland computer utility. ISD has a proprietary computer program which affords them considerable advantage in selling shared-time computer services to major sophisticated users. This program, which had been protected as proprietary by due warning to employees and customers, enables ISD to use standard telephone "modems" for plotting or graphing computer output at the customer's remote terminal location. The program also provides the capability of punched paper tape output at customer's site.

Access to ISD's computer (basically, a Univac 1108 with associated peripheral equipment) was standard for this type of computer utility or a proprietary computer center; customers (remote terminals) have an unlisted telephone number to dial and a code number to enter at their terminal which will simultaneously identify the terminal to the computer and give the remote terminal access to operate the computer. In other words, given a telephone number and an authorized code number, the ISD computer — very typically — could be accessed, instructions given, the computer operated, and the results returned to whomever was calling at wherever the call was coming from. With direct dialing in effect throughout virtually the entire United States and much of Canada, this call could have almost as readily been made from a public telephone booth in Canada.[2] The customer whose code was used would, of course, be billed for the time used, and in this case was billed, but the amount of computer time involved in the unauthorized acquisition was so small it

---

The details of the first case on legal record of a computer's having been accessed by an unauthorized computer terminal. The catastrophically simple method used, the detection, and the preliminary investigation.

---

approached "invisibility" as a billing. The civil complaint details the time and duration of access and the amount billed; the total time billed (for accessing the computer three times, punching 515 cards, and printing 15 pages at the remote location) was six *seconds,* and the customer was billed $2.54. Not unaturally, the customer had no questions about the billing.

Recognizing the responsibility of storing customers' data on its own

---

[1] *While considered to be commercially improbable, this risk has not been considered improbable in defense and proprietary computer operation and storage. Defense research and development facilities, particularly, have been incorporating defenses against surreptitious access for at least a decade.*

[2] *While this possibility is hopefully more remote, it requires only the same degree of sophistication and computer availability.*

premises, ISD offers customers an encrypting service for the protection of ISD-stored proprietary information. Data stored encrypted can be "read out" in clear only upon receipt of a code word known to the customer's authorized employes, and not known at ISD. In other words, an instruction to print out the encrypted information by an unauthorized person, which would include ISD personnel, would only produce what would appear to be gibberish.

A parallel protection for basic computer programs, such as the "purloined" proprietary program, is a basic computer "instruction" for the computer to respond negatively to any order to print out, revise, or erase some or all of the computer's basic routines. The instruction could be implemented in a number of ways, or combination of ways; it could be implemented by automatically disconnecting the terminal making the attempt, by printing out at the computer console the fact that the routine has been called up and is waiting an "approved" command, or any of several other very simple (for a computer) routines. This protection ISD had not incorporated, having anticipated no need for it.

DISCOVERY

Under the circumstances, it is not surprising that ISD learned of the unauthorized acquisition almost by chance, when a customer returned punched cards prepared by ISD, which the customer denied ordering. These were the 515 punched cards produced in response to the first access (of three) on the night in question. These cards had been, as a matter of routine, delivered to the customer by courier promptly after their production at ISD's facility. When the punched cards had been retrieved from the customer, they were printed out, in an effort to identify the "error." The card run reproduced ISD's highly proprie-

tary PLOT/TRANS program, printing the computer instructions for the program in 489 lines requiring 11 pages. Going to billing records, ISD discovered the order to punch the cards was received at 6:15:20 p.m. on January 19, 1971. At 6:17:20 the same customer code number was used to access the computer a second time, this time — according to computer records for billing — producing 489 lines and 11 pages at the "customer's" remote location. (A third access, at 6:23:15, read 110 cards at the "customer's" location, used one second of computer time, and printed seven lines, indicating an unsuccessful attempt for an undeterminable purpose.)

It appeared certain that the PLOT/TRANS program had been abstracted deliberately and successfully. In seeking the cause, ISD had occasion to settle their attention rather early on a nearby computer utility, University Computing Company, of Palo Alto. Among the matters which sharpened their interest in this possibility were: The customer code used in the acquisition was the same at both ISD *and* UCC, a fact known to both computer utilities, and arranged as a courtesy to, and at the request of, the customer in question, who felt it would be less confusing if they could have the same calling number at each computer utility servicing the facility. Secondly, UCC's basic computer is also a Univac 1108, which would help simplify certain necessary analyses. Further, UCC competed directly with ISD for the same customers, and an affidavit filed in support of the resulting civil action states that UCC personnel had told personnel of a common customer that UCC would shortly have the same remote plotting capability, and that UCC could access ISD's computer "anytime they wanted to."

In addition, UCC had a significant remoting capability which ISD did not; this was the ability to punch cards at the customer's location. In other words, a command to ISD's computer to punch cards at the customer's location would be interpreted by the ISD equipment as an instruction to punch cards *at the computer center*, as did indeed occur. A similar instruction given to UCC's computer would have produced punched cards at the *customer's location*, which must logically have been the purpose of the first access/command.

ISD executives sought police assistance in identifying the telephone call or calls by which the computer had been accessed at the times in question. Since the telephone company required specific telephone numbers both to and from, to perform the check, it took some time to find the correct combination of many possibilities. The call was found to have been placed to an unlisted ISD number from UCC's dataphone. The call was found to have lasted 11 minutes, 32 seconds, and corresponded precisely to the time of the unauthorized computer runs, according to the affidavit.

On February 17, 1971, an officer of ISD, together with Sgt. Green of the Oakland Police Department and others, met with representatives of the Alameda County District Attorney's Office.[3] The deputy district attorneys consulted concluded sufficient grounds existed to justify a warrant to search the premises of UCC in Palo Alto, and the residence of an employee of UCC (the person named in the criminal complaint). The search warrant was sought and obtained in Santa Clara County on February 19.

---

[3] *Oakland is located in Alameda County; Palo Alto, in Santa Clara County. Criminal charges, under PC499 C, California's Trade Secrets Act, have been filed in Alameda County; a civil suit is pending in Santa Clara County. The bulk of the information here is drawn from the civil complaint file.*

At the request of the Alameda District Attorney's Office, ISD provided a representative "skilled in computer programming" to accompany the search. It is reliably reported that a neutral source, similarly skilled, was also asked to be, and was, present as an impartial advisor. The request for such personnel arose from the fact that the warrant was unprecedented in its extent and the technicality of the fruits of the search; quite literally, the most experienced investigators could not have fully performed the search called for, without having such expertise available to them.

THE SEARCH

The search warrant, which was issued pursuant to the criminal charges, authorized a search of the personal property of the employee, both at his residence and at University Computing Company, and the premises of University Computing Company, for: "One, keypunch computer cards punched with Information Systems Design's remote plotting program; two, computer printout sheets with printouts of Information Systems Design's remote plotting program; and, three, computer memory banks or other data storage devices magnetically imprinted with Information Systems Design's remote plotting computer program." The unprecedented extent of the search warrant lies most distinctly in the third "area" of search. UCC is reported to have, among other memory devices, two FASTRAND magnetic drums, each capable of holding approximately 132 million characters. These, of course, are in addition to disc, tape, and a large core memory. All of the memory devices were read out in the course of the search, which took approximately nine hours. The fruits of the search of the memory are presumed to be in the nine 2400-ft. reels of magnetic tape (which store information at 800 bits/inch) which are listed on the property receipt.

Among physical property listed in the civil complaint affidavit as having been recovered in the search of the employee's office at UCC were: a handwritten note telling how to access ISD's computer; a photocopy of an instruction sheet ISD gives its customers on how to utilize ISD's remote plotting capability; an unlisted ISD telephone number provided only to ISD customers, written on a piece of paper; a binder marked "ISD" containing (among others) printouts of a computer run made on ISD's computer but printed on UCC's particular type of computer paper, apparently on UCC's output device;[4] and a printout of a computer program, which was found on a table in the defendant's office. The affidavit in the civil case states, in regard to this last, "Affiant recognized [the program] immediately as similar to ISD's remote plotting program suspected to have been stolen. Affiant examined the first one-third of the program and found a line-for-line and character-for-character correspondence in at least 75% of the lines. At the request of UCC officials, further examination of that program was deferred."

Also recovered in the search, according to a property receipt, were six handwritten pages, paper-clipped, labeled "ISD message format," as well as substantial numbers of pages of information and manuals provided by ISD to its customers. The name of a second common customer of the two computer utilities enters in the description of the fruits of the search, and the civil case affidavit charges the defendant had access to ISD proprietary equipment at the customer's site.[5]

OUTCOME

At the time of writing, nothing has evolved beyond a temporary court order restraining UCC from divulging any information or providing any of the services which the firm did not have prior to the compromise of ISD's system.

Whatever the outcome of either the civil or the criminal action — and the criminal case represents the first charges brought under this particular section of the California Code — this precedent-setting case will, as it should, stimulate in customers of computer utilities, computer utilities themselves, and proprietary central computer center administrators, substantial new interest in line security, data storage security, computer billings, and the protection of basic programs.

It is ironic that the entire breach could not have occurred if a simple computer routine had been standard operating practice: If, when signalled by a customer code, the computer automatically disconnected the call and dialed the customer identified, it could not have happened as it did.

But it did happen, and it could happen at most commercial computer centers in the United States today. ∎

---

[4] *The output of a computer utility is distinctive because of billing information and other internal codes, etc., which are incorporated in the printout, while the paper on which the output is printed is, in standard practice, purchased with the name of the company incorporated in it. In addition, printers — that is, automatic typing devices which print out the computer transmission — are distinctive precisely as typewriters are distinctive, by minute or gross differences in wear, angle, pressure, etc.*

[5] *An unofficial inquiry to the second customer from Security World indicates that both vendors had proprietary equipment in the same area at the customer's site, and that defendant's presence in the area was, generally, authorized and unremarkable.*

> After press time, UCC filed an answer to the civil suit, arguing that ISD's program was not unique, denying that UCC lacked such a program, and stating that ISD had been aware UCC had accessed ISD's computer at other times. In addition, UCC has filed a cross-suit charging defamation... [as of May, 1971]

A Practical Handbook For Computer Facility Security

by Charles F. Hemphill, Jr.

A 'security checklist' is provided for an effective program of loss prevention in and around the computer...understandable to management and security director alike, this straightforward summary touches on vital points of vulnerability, alerts to critical problems.

INTRODUCTION

Within the span of only a few years, the computer has become the rather commonplace, but vital, nerve center of business. Increasingly, firms of all kinds have become more dependent upon EDP records.

Yet no individual factor in trade or industry can surpass the computer in its potential to harm an entire business! This factor has been recognized to be so critical that failure to take essential steps to protect computer records can result in the personal liability of corporation directors to company stockholders.

An effective program for preventing loss of computer records incorporates the combined skills of management, company employed computer professionals, and the corporate official with responsibility for loss prevention or security.

Most firms have also found that it is necessary to have a written program with established procedural rules. In addition, management must demand strict computer supervision and make regular reviews and audits of procedures. The loss prevention director must also insure that security hazards do not develop in day to day operations.

SECURITY CHECKLIST

The establishment of an effective computer security program should be based upon a number of important considerations.

Facility Location

Where possible, every effort should be made to locate the computer facility in a relatively crime free neighborhood — where employees feel safe reporting to work at all hours of the day or night. The proximity of emergency support facilities, such as fire and police protection, should also be considered.

Building Construction

Many physical catastrophies can be avoided through proper planning. Flooding, either from an overflowing waterway or from bursting water pipes in the building, are among the potential disasters that must be avoided. Planning is also advisable to reduce the likelihood of a serious gas explosion. Building collapse is another hazard. Structures must be capable of supporting substantial weight.

If costly computer equipment and records are maintained in a well constructed building, management may also avoid many of the possibilities of loss through hurricane, tornado, and other natural disasters.

Fire Protection

Destruction by fire may be by far the most devastating of all environmental hazards. Insurance figures maintained for a number of years in the United States reflect that approximately one-half of all firms sustaining loss of records through fire are unable to continue in business.

It is therefore essential that computer protection should emphasize fire detection systems, fire suppressant systems, and employee training in use and verification of detection and suppressant systems.

Physical Security

To make certain that unauthorized individuals do not penetrate into sensitive areas, an effective computer security program makes good use of physical security.

At the minimum, planning should be directed toward adequate lighting, fencing, locks, alarms, and guard systems. Consideration must be given to controlling access through doors, windows, vent shafts, dumb-waiter shafts, entry from adjoining buildings, and other possibilities. Techniques and procedures must also be in effect to keep unwanted intruders out.

Back-Up Systems

Since all man-made machines will eventually fail, an effective program should include the preparation of back-up systems. It has been found through trial and error that it is necessary to utilize regular 'dry runs' of computer back-up systems after they have been designed. Unless this precaution is taken the plan may prove to be unworkable when it is most needed — in a time of emergency.

At the minimum, there are three kinds of back-up capability that must be considered:

(1) Machine (computer processor) capability. Actual tests show that the computer hardware that is relied on for a back-up system may not be compatible, unless tests are made.

(2) Air conditioning back-up to make certain that required temperature conditions can be maintained in the event of failure of the system.

(3) Back-up electrical power. This usually involves the installation and testing of a back-up generator — with an adequate fuel supply, protected in such a way that the back-up generator would function if the usual source of power should be sabotaged or lost.

Protection of Records

Ordinary business safes are not adequate to protect computer tapes or disks against fire damage. Accordingly, consideration should be given to acquiring and using special computer safes. Experience shows, however, that unless procedures are carefully set up and followed, safes of this kind may not be locked or secured when an emergency arises. Accordingly, procedures to verify proper use must be instituted as well.

Another basic security precaution involves the use of an off-site storage location for back-up tapes or disks. This should include master files of the third generation or 'grandfather' type, along with operating systems software back-up. It is also valuable to set up — in writing — retention instructions pertaining to all vital records, with clearly defined procedures for auditing the implementation of such instructions.

Access Controls to the Computer

Control of access to the computer and to adjoining support areas is also vital. Adequate locking devices are essential, with a double-door entry concept, controlled by an employee in the computer room. Entry authority should be controlled and verified, and consideration given to the use of badge systems or other controls to prevent unauthorized access to vital areas inside the computer installation proper.

Remote Terminal Access

If remote terminals are utilized, techniques and controls should be set up to make certain that unauthorized individuals cannot gain access to the computer through these terminals. If desirable, lockword techniques and other controls may be utilized, depending on the particular installation.

Operational Considerations

Operating programs should be maintained under lock and key by supervision. Definite procedures should be set up and audited to make certain that NO programs are modified, documented, or utilized without authority.

It is also considered essential that there be a basic separation between operators and programmers. Master file changes should originate in the appropriate department of the business and there should be definite controls prohibiting computer personnel from making unauthorized modifications.

Additional controls may be desirable in operating areas. A log giving details of machine halts and the problems encountered that cause them should be maintained and regularly reviewed by supervising management.

Tape Library Controls

An effective program should incorporate basic controls for the issuance and use of tapes or disks, and logs should be maintained and audited.

It is suggested that time on the computer also be audited to make certain that computer employees are not allowed to operate their own business on the company equipment.

Controls should be set up to preclude the theft or duplication of program documentation or records.

Disposal Problems

Plans should be made for disposal of stored information, records, printouts, *etc.*, after each is no longer needed. Unless adequate procedures are set up and enforced, confidential tapes or disks that are presumed destroyed may become available to outside persons.

Often a paper shredder may be utilized, or burning procedures worked out. Precautions should be taken to make certain that carbon paper from continuous printout forms is not available to unauthorized persons.

Internal Auditing Procedures

There should also be a capability for internal auditing procedures, with one or more members of the staff capable of writing and understanding programs. Test data for financial accounting should be regularly furnished to employees with auditing responsibility, accompanied by copies and updates of all program documentation.

Emergency Shutdown and Recovery Procedures

Actual cases have demonstrated that it is highly desirable to prepare an emergency shutdown program specifically designed for the individual computer installation.

Here, also, it is recommended that a 'dry run' of the program be made and rechecked from time to time. Such 'dry runs' enable responsible security personnel to make certain that protective devices continue to be available and functional and that both old and new employees understand their responsibilities in the event of an emergency shutdown.

It is important that employee responsibilities and supervisory authority of this program are spelled out in detail and carefully explained to all those involved.

In addition, experience demonstrates that sufficient emergency records should be available to set up a recovery program that will get the business back into operation in the quickest possible time.

Employee Hiring

Because of the great potential it offers for disaster from seemingly small acts, only individuals of proven reliability should be hired for jobs related to the computer.

Management should also continue to audit and control the performance of individuals during their time of employment.

Legal Protection

Possible legal problems with, and all legal aspects of, computer contracts and leasing should be studied.

It is also suggested that legal advice be obtained in the area of protecting company trade secrets, and in assessing the possibility of copyrighting or patenting some aspects of company records and procedures.

In order to protect computer secrets, signed 'non-compete' agreements should be requested from employees.

MILITANTS AND PUBLIC TOURS

Management should have an understanding of the hazards that have been created in the past by militant groups. While it is hoped that the destructive activities of these organizations have now passed, the threats posed by vandalism and anti-establishment destruction cannot be completely overlooked. Further, employee procedures and physical protective devices should be maintained at a high level at all times, to insure that unauthorized persons are kept out. Individuals with good intentions can sometimes cause accidental problems in the computer room, and if someone with a grudge against the computer installation is allowed to enter, then the best of access controls may be nullified. Tours may be a source of entry for malicious persons, as well as many well-intentioned who cause accidents. Therefore, it is recommended that public tours not be allowed through the computer area. If carefully selected groups are allowed inside, they should be furnished an adequate escort and kept appropriately distant from equipment.

COMPUTER INSURANCE

Regular insurance policies do not provide the kinds of coverage that may be needed by a business that maintains its records on computer. An initial program that will evaluate the specific business needs of every business is therefore recommended.

Additional insurance may be needed that provides protection against damage and destruction to computers and equipment — including damage by fire, explosion, wind, water, smoke, accidental damage, building collapse, vandalism, electrical destruction, land movement, or shock waves.

Study should also be given to insurance coverage for tapes that might be lost, stolen, or damaged through malicious acts. Disks, cards, media, and manuals should also be included for protection against this kind of loss.

Other computer insurance coverages may also be advisable, such as extra expense insurance that is not a normal business coverage, third party liability, and time sharing loss. If data files and programs are regularly taken off the premises, additional insurance protection may be needed to prevent loss in transit or at the alternate location.

Also, errors and omissions coverage may be needed if work is performed for outsiders. Employee bonding and honesty insurance may also be worthwhile under those conditions.

PROTECTION OF NEGOTIABLES

An adequate security program will also take into account the loss potential represented by revenue-producing forms, checks, or other negotiable instruments generated by the computer. Study should also be given to those procedures that are used for the printing of payroll and accounts payable checks, and for controlling negotiable documents after issuance.

COMMENT

The security needs of a computer installation will vary from place to place, and from firm to firm. In addition to the protective measures that have been outlined here, additional controls may be designed to fit the needs of the individual installation. ∎

Since its founding in 1964, **Security World** magazine, from whose pages this booklet is drawn, has been — and is — a primary influence in the professionalization of security. Besides the magazine, which goes to 185,000 regular readers in the United States, Canada, and more than twenty other countries, Security World sponsors the International Security Conference, three annual meetings on professional security, with which are associated the world's largest exhibits of security equipment.

The editor of "Computer Security," June-Elizabeth Thorsen, is editor-in-chief of **Security World** magazine. She joined Security World Publishing Co. in 1971. Ms. Thorsen has been multi-media editor for a major educational publisher, managing editor of another national magazine, director with a large national association, and has taught communications and journalism-related subjects at two state universities.